# CORNISH PIRATES

## LEGENDS

### STEVE TOMLIN

AMBERLEY

First published 2015

Amberley Publishing
The Hill, Stroud
Gloucestershire, GL5 4EP

www.amberley-books.com

British Library Cataloguing in Publication Data.
A catalogue record for this book is available from the British Library.

ISBN 978 1 4456 4656 5 (print)
ISBN 978 1 4456 4657 2 (ebook)

Typesetting and Origination by Amberley Publishing.
Printed in the UK.

# ABOUT THE AUTHOR

Steve Tomlin was born and bred on a farm near Penzance. He began to follow the Pirates at the age of nine so beginning a life-long devotion of nearly sixty years.

Despite lengthy periods away at university and with his career he somehow managed nearly 150 games for the club as a prop-forward and around fifty more for their Colts team. In recent years he has contributed regularly to the club's website and programme notes as 'Old Prop Steve' and for six years acted as a summariser on BBC local radio whenever the Pirates travelled outside of Cornwall.

A retired HR director in the pharmaceutical industry, he now lives with his wife Miquette near his family and grandchildren in Hertfordshire but still travels regularly back to Cornwall to watch his beloved Cornish Pirates.

This is his second book about the club having published *Pirates! Pirates!* in 2009.

Pirates 1946–47. This picture includes John Kendall-Carpenter (standing, on right, six people in), John 'Ginger' Williams (seated, second in from right) and seated on the ground on the right Harvey Richards

# CONTENTS

**Note:** Appearances and tries refer to first team matches only but include all 'friendlies' as well as league and cup matches. In the amateur era the club usually ran two or three teams and so players from that time often played in considerably more matches for the club than are reflected here.

During the 1980s the club sometimes failed to keep detailed records of their match day line-ups and the local press usually only provided results and try scorers. As a result two or three players from that era may have their number of matches played and tries scored underestimated.

# INTRODUCTION

A certain amount of controversy has never worried me unduly, although in Cornwall you never have to go very far to find it.

The only job in rugby I have never taken on – and now I know why – was as a selector. One thing that is guaranteed is that nobody will ever agree entirely with anyone else regarding any list of fifty remarkable men who have all graced the colours of Penzance and Newlyn RFC and its latter day incarnation as the Cornish Pirates. I can already hear people muttering 'What on earth is so-and-so doing in there?' or 'How could he ever leave out our Jimmy?'

I will plead in my defence that with the obvious exception of Barrie Bennetts, an extraordinary man who played for Penzance RFC before the First World War, I have actually met and watched in action virtually every one of the men contained in this book at some point in my life. Indeed I also had the privilege of playing alongside a few of them and commented upon many others on the radio so I suppose my choices are probably just about as valid as those of the next person.

I have included four leading coaches each of whom can lay claim to having had a profound influence not only upon the fortunes of the Pirates themselves but also on the developing careers of large numbers of professional players dotted around the world.

A second point of controversy will probably reverberate about the name of the team and hence the title of this book. The rebranding of the club in 2005 as the Cornish Pirates was accepted by most but derided by many and there will undoubtedly be some celebrated in here who will always regard themselves as Penzance and Newlyn men until the day they die. Nevertheless this has been written in 2015 for a current rugby-loving readership and as they say 'we are where we are'.

The history of the Pirates can be divided roughly into four phases. Newlyn and Penzance each ran separate clubs for over fifty years up until the Second World War with neither ever seriously challenging the dominance of the two teams at the heart of Cornwall – namely Redruth and, to a slightly lesser extent, Camborne.

The arrival of peace in 1945 saw not only an amalgamation of the two old and sometimes bitter rivals but also the discovery of a rich seam of talented players. They were backed by both an ambitious committee and a huge local following which thronged the touchlines at the newly constructed Mennaye Field. There were far fewer counter attractions in that era of post-war austerity, the club flourished and a great time was had by all.

That initial burst of success began to wane in the late 1960s and for the next twenty-five years the club itself and the various teams it fielded went into a prolonged period of relative decline. Certainly there were still some very good players, who were often also devoted club men, but the results on the pitch, attendances at matches and the quality of fixtures all declined alarmingly. This is reflected by the fact that only a handful of players from that era have been included.

In the mid-1990s rugby belatedly accepted the principle of paying players. It is doubtful whether anyone in Cornwall at the time seriously contemplated professional rugby applying in the remote and often parochial Duchy. The Pirates had however gained the patronage of an enthusiastic former player named Richard Evans who had made his fortune establishing a vegetable and horticultural conglomerate in East Africa. New and exciting players were attracted to the club who thus gained five promotions in only eight years to emerge as a fully professional championship outfit. Once there they faced many of the top clubs in the land while winning trophies and reaching playoffs along the way. Inevitably the men of this period represent the lion's share of this book.

When I first watched the Pirates as a young boy in the 1950s the players seemed to be almost God-like figures to me and so the opportunity to meet some of them again and to wallow in unashamed nostalgia for those days long past was a great thrill. My own first hero was a strapping blond winger called Geoff Vingoe who does not appear in these pages. I was about eight years old and sitting on the grass by the side of the pitch when he was hurled into touch and very nearly landed on top of me. He looked down and grinned and winked at me before running back onto the field. Sixty years later I am still in awe of him!

Constructing this book has been a fascinating experience as I had the chance to meet and interview nearly all of the men in question either face to face, by telephone or via Skype. Every single person I approached has been incredibly helpful, keen to assist and extremely kind. I had half expected at least someone to tell me to get lost but nobody ever did. Some of the older players have inevitably passed away but in that case I have had the invaluable help of their former colleagues or family members and friends who have all done their very best to help me.

The lifestyles of those amateur players and that of the modern Cornish Pirates are very different. The standards of fitness, size, skills, power, tactics, medical attention and preparation are light years apart. It is gratifying, however, to see just how many of the old positive values engendered by rugby remain mercifully intact. Despite their many achievements, the old qualities of self-deprecating humour, loyalty, courtesy and a disarming modesty were universal despite the fact that their ages ranged from twenty-five to ninety.

Rugby is still not a sport which generates very much money and there is no question that the great majority of today's players still play primarily for the love of the game. Indeed most of the amateur players received relatively better incomes and security from their day jobs and certainly enjoyed more multi-dimensional lifestyles than their modern equivalents – especially those now performing in the premiership.

Professional rugby players have inevitably been forced to put their longer term careers on hold for at least a decade and are all acutely conscious of the fact that they are always just a bad tackle away from, not only an abrupt end to their rugby playing days, but possibly a difficult trip to the job centre as well. For all that no doubt we should all have loved to have stepped into their shoes.

I have enjoyed a great deal of help from many people in putting this book together. Firstly from each and every one of the players and coaches themselves and also from my old friend Phil Westren at the Cornish Pirates whose huge collection of Pirates memorabilia is matched only by his enthusiastic and generous willingness to somehow find me whatever I needed. I would also like to record my appreciation and gratitude to Graham Nicholas, Geoff Vingoe, Jane Stevens, Mary Tudor, Mike Richards, David Mann, Ian Connell, Graham Dawe, Paul Jenkin, Sue Pascoe, Roger Roberts, Anita George, Jan Rendall, Jimmy Reid and Dicky Evans as well as Brian Tempest, Mike Cox, Martin Bennett and Simon Bryant for their kind permission to use their photographs. My thanks also go out to Tom Poad and Vanessa Le at Amberley Publishing for all their guidance and encouragement.

Steve Tomlin
Berkhamsted, 2015

# CHAPTER ONE

# THE COACHES

## Ian Davies

Position: Coach / Director of Rugby
Date of Birth: 1973
Playing Career: Llanelli Juniors New Dock
Stars

Did you know? Ian has played cricket against Viv Richards and Gordon Greenidge.

Ian Davies was born at Morriston near Swansea but brought up in Llanelli. His family were not a keen rugby household but if you grow up in the old tinplate town you are inevitably immersed in it.

He started playing rugby while at primary school and played in the juniors with local club New Dock Stars and Llanelli. He was keen on all sport and had a PE teacher named Nick Murphy who clearly had an impact upon Ian and the direction he was to take in life. Apart from rugby he was a very promising young cricketer which he played at junior county level.

He entered the Llanelli Schools team where one of his colleagues was Scott Quinnell and at that time was destined to join the police force. He had terrible luck and suffered two serious spinal injuries and two knee dislocations, so his playing career was over almost before it had begun. It also put paid to his joining the police.

He then decided to train for the teaching profession and that willingness to impart knowledge and develop young people naturally led him towards sports coaching. He had toyed with the idea of refereeing and actually attended courses with a youthful

Nigel Owens. He also considered going to university in Cardiff. However, when the chance came to studying at Chichester University and coaching rugby at the same time, he jumped at the chance. Once he had graduated he was appointed their Director of Student Sport.

He then had a spell teaching science at the Bishop Luffa School in Chichester and working with the Sussex rugby squads where one of his young players was the future England prop Joe Marler. He also once coached Sussex against Cornwall in a county match at Redruth.

He then did an MSc in Enhancing and Maintaining Elite Performance at the University of Portsmouth. Meanwhile his coaching experience began to expand with the South of England Students who went on to win the inter-regional competition in each of the four years he was in charge.

He had already gained his Level Three coaching badge but went on to obtain the much more demanding Level Four. He also became Director of Rugby for Worthing RFC and took them up to the National Three Level – a position they had never attained in the past.

He crossed paths with the Cornish Pirates when he founded a sevens team known as the Scorpions who were essentially ex-Chichester University students who played throughout the UK and in venues like Biarritz, Marbella and Benidorm. They met a strong Pirates team at the Henley Sevens, beat them and then went on to lift the trophy. As the Pirates were the holders from the previous year the significance was not lost upon them.

In 2009 Chris Stirling was coming to Cornwall and was looking for both backs and forwards specialist coaches so Ian put in an application. The Pirates were a couple of notches above where he had worked to date but his credentials were impressive and one afternoon, as he was preparing Worthing for a match, a man approached him and handed him his business card. It was Dicky Evans.

Soon he had become part of a coaching trinity of Stirling, Ian himself and the ex-Blackheath coach Harvey Biljon. The trio made an instant impact bringing a massively enhanced professional approach to organisation, preparation, conditioning and tactical awareness. Stirling took most of the plaudits but Ian was doing a tremendous amount of work behind the scenes – not only on the training paddock but in detailed analysis as well. This is now standard practice at all senior rugby clubs but in 2009–10 this was taken to a new level as far as the Pirates were concerned.

The team began well and then stuttered in the championship. They had suffered badly with injuries and for a time concerted scrum and other set piece work was proving virtually impossible. In November the Pirates made their first ever trip to Ireland to face Leinster A at Donnybrook and suddenly the scrum seemed to step up a level. Ian had brought a very strong loose-head prop called Ryan Storer with him from Worthing and he, alongside two other 'newbies' in Ward and Rimmer, dominated a Leinster pack which included Irish internationals Jack McGrath and the giant Devin Toner. The Pirates lost the match on some debatable refereeing decisions but by then Ian's influence was plain to see.

The next three years saw unprecedented success with the British & Irish Cup being won, the team qualifying for every playoff and reaching two championship finals. Several forwards saw their careers take a huge leap forward including not only Ward and Rimmer but also Ian Nimmo, Chris Morgan, Sam Betty, Mike Myerscough and Phil Burgess to name just a few. Furthermore several experienced men like Alan Paver, Laurie McGlone, Rob Elloway and Ben Gulliver seemed to step up to greater levels of fitness and performance.

None of this happened by accident. If Ian was at heart a teacher he was one who was hard but fair, uncompromising but flexible, tactically astute but would wear that teacher's heart on his sleeve. He had a good network of contacts and seemed to revel in taking a talented twenty-one-year-old from somewhere like Loughborough, Hartbury or a National III club and moulding him to meet the often physically brutal demands of the championship and beyond.

Early in 2012 Chris Stirling indicated his wish to return to New Zealand. This was undoubtedly a blow and his organisational and man management skills would clearly be hard to follow but Evans was in no doubt that he already had the man to step up already present, willing and waiting. The situation Ian inherited was not without its difficulties. Hopes for a publicly funded stadium for Cornwall had been cruelly dashed by the county council the previous May and, on the back of this, many of the squad which had been so painstakingly assembled over the previous three seasons had been snapped up by premiership clubs.

He managed to sign a few experienced campaigners – among them Tom Riley, Kieran Hallett, Ben Prescott and Gary Johnson. He had also forged a strong link with Exeter Chiefs and as a result several outstandingly talented youngsters gained some invaluable experience in the championship including Sam Hill, Jack Nowell, Jack Yeandle and, most notably, Dave Ewers. For eighteen months he continued to work in tandem with Harvey Biljon. The club finished a creditable sixth in their first season and made the quarter-finals of the B & I cup when Munster returned to Cornwall and gained revenge for their defeat three years previously.

The following Christmas Biljon landed the top job at Jersey and was on his way. Ian moved up from being the senior of the duo to take over fully as Director of Rugby and was soon joined by Gavin Cattle and Alan Paver as player/coaches who each had to make the transition towards an entirely new way of working.

Ian and his young family settled happily into Cornwall and have been there for six years. He naturally harbours ambitions to coach at a Premiership or Pro 12 club but derives his greatest job satisfaction in seeing young talented players develop.

If that indicates the instinct of the teacher and mentor innate within him it should also be said that for Ian a real pleasure is a lazy summer's day spent watching a really good game of cricket.

# Jim McKay

Position: Chief Coach
Date of Birth: 1966
Playing Career: Warringah, Gordon, Randwick, Stourbridge, North Walsham

Did you know? While surfing in Indonesia Jim once spent several weeks living in a cave at Ulluwattu.

Jim McKay always seemed destined to be a rugby coach. Even when growing up in the sports-mad city of Sydney he seemed to enjoy organising almost as much as playing. He was brought up on a diet of Australia's different sports including cricket, touch rugby, football, Rugby League and Rugby Union. Jim's other passion was surfing which has remained with him ever since.

His senior playing career began at a local Sydney club named Warringah which he described as a very forward-orientated club before linking up with Randwick which, as one of the leading rugby clubs in the Southern Hemisphere, is famous for its running rugby philosophy.

Jim was a winger and occasional fullback in a side bristling with famous Wallabies including David Campese, Simon Poidevin, Phil Kearns and the Ella brothers. In fact Jim was one of only a few members of that team never to have been capped by Australia. In all, he made approximately 100 First Grade appearances in the New South Wales premier grade competition.

Even more significantly he worked and played alongside some of the most innovative coaches of that and future eras such as Bob Dwyer, Rod Macqueen, Alan Gaffney, Ewen McKenzie, Eddie Jones and Michael Chieka.

Rugby was still amateur and he trained as a carpenter but often got himself into trouble with his supervisor for talking too much. 'Less yap, yap and more tap, tap please McKay,' he was told on one occasion. Jim's ambitions however soared far above the workbench and he was keen to see the world and to play and coach some rugby while doing so.

He had already spent time travelling in Nepal, Indonesia and even a period picking avocados on a kibbutz in Israel.

A mutual contact in the UK was a man named Jon Collins. It was he who pointed Jim towards Stourbridge where he was able to both play and implement some of the coaching methods he had already learned despite still being only twenty-four years old. He then moved to East Anglia playing and coaching with Norwich and North Walsham. Compared with life back at Randwick he found attitudes towards fitness, drinking and tactics were distinctly rustic. But in time he got his message across and both clubs enjoyed getting promoted far beyond where they might once have ever thought possible.

He was then ready to coach full-time and took the job at Henley Hawks where Sir Clive Woodward had cut his coaching teeth only a few years previously. In his four years at Dry Leas they gained two promotions and Jim was then invited to lead Orrell's push for promotion back to the premiership. That team included several future Pirates including Gavin Cattle, Richard Welding, Peter Ince and Wade Kelly plus England's Nick Easter. Having lost out narrowly to Worcester the owner promptly took all his money away and left the club high and dry.

He, Cattle and the others transferred to Rotherham but, when that club immediately suffered precisely the same fate, he was contacted by Dicky Evans initially to assist Kevin Moseley as a backs coach. Moseley had taken the Pirates up three levels but had not found championship level rugby easy and thus, after a disappointing defeat at Sedgeley Park, McKay took over his job.

Jim brought several talented players to Penzance including Cattle, Welding, Heino Senekal, Joe Beardshaw and the exciting Alberto di Bernardo as well as the scrum coach Robin Cowling and the Kiwi conditioning man Simon Raynes. He was at pains to develop a philosophy of how the game should be approached and put great emphasis upon developing younger players even if this entailed them eventually moving on elsewhere.

His highlight was undoubtedly the EDF Trophy win at Twickenham, which he recalls as one of the most memorable coaching events in his career. The journey from the dressing room up to the bar under the stand took nearly an hour as he was mobbed repeatedly by Pirates fans wanting to feel, hold and have their pictures taken with the trophy. The climax was when he finally handed it over to Dicky Evans saying something like 'this is for you mate'. Jim has had many big moments at Super 14 and international level since then but that memory even today still burns deep in his soul.

A number of Pirates moved on after that season and a surprisingly-relegated Northampton Saints looked to run away with the championship. In fact the Pirates had three cracking matches with them but, after the third, it was announced that Jim was leaving. The club had just been through one of its many false dawns regarding the stadium at Truro, a frustrated Evans had himself stepped down from the presidency and the pressures had all become enormous.

Jim moved out to be replaced by his forwards coach Mark Hewitt and for a while he coached at Redruth and Truro College before joining the Leicester Tigers Academy. Before long he returned to Australia to assume the role of Senior Assistant Coach of the Queensland Reds for four years 2010–2013 where the highlight was seeing the side being crowned Super Rugby Champions in 2011 and developing such players as Quade

Cooper and Will Genia. During this time he completed his master's degree in Coaching and Education at Sydney University having enrolled at the age of forty.

In 2013 it was announced that he would join Ewen McKenzie and the Wallabies as attack coach where he had some exceptionally talented men to work with. One of his fondest memories of that time was seeing his old Pirates fly-half Alberto di Bernardo playing for Italy against the Wallabies in Turin. However, the Wallabies could not dislodge the All Blacks from their pinnacle of world rugby and in time one of those recurring palace revolutions which seem to happen in international sport resulted in the entire coaching team being ousted – including Jim.

He recently had a spell with Worcester Warriors in a consultancy role but has undoubtedly fallen in love with Cornwall and the lure of the sea and the surf led to his buying a house at Newquay which he still retains. Jim is a regular visitor to Cornwall and remains open minded about coming back to live the Cornish life once again – and of course coach some rugby.

# Kevin Moseley

Position: Lock later Head Coach
Height/Weight: 6' 7", 19st 6lbs
Date of Birth: 1963
Matches: 85 + 3
Tries: 8

Did you know? In an interview with *The Rugby Paper* the giant Welsh enforcer claimed to have been bullied at school.

Kevin Moseley was born in Caerphilly but brought up in nearby Blackwood in a close-knit mining area where rugby has always been a major feature of daily life. He went to school in nearby Oakdale and then Pontllanfraith – a cradle of many Welsh rugby legends including the great Alun Pask.

His brother was a rugby player but Kevin, although very tall, was a gangly lad who was not very interested in sport. This all changed when he took up the game at seventeen mainly to be in with his mates. When he eventually got going he made rapid strides with Blackwood Colts although he had to start from scratch by learning the Rugby Laws. He was helped by a man called Sid Bisp and soon got into the senior Blackwood team which played mighty Cardiff in a cup match. After the game Cardiff showed interest but he was also spotted by Pontypool and joined them in 1983.

At that time 'Pooler' was the dominant force in Welsh rugby and in that first season carried all before them by winning forty-six of their fifty fixtures and scoring some 1,607 points in doing so. The team was led by BBC commentator Eddie Butler and included some genuinely hard men such as Jeff Squire, Bobby Windsor, Jeff Perkins, Staff Jones, Chris Huish and the great Graham Price. Furthermore it was coached by the extraordinary ex-British Lion prop Ray Prosser who gave Kevin his nickname of 'Boris' when he once appeared with stitches in his face and apparently reminded Prosser of Boris Karloff.

The term 'legend' is grossly overused but stories about Prosser in Welsh rugby are legion. He was in some ways a rugby equivalent of Bill Shankly – no tactical genius but would send men out on a pitch prepared to die for the cause. It was a very tough school but Kevin learned fast

For the next four years the club's pre-eminence in Wales continued. They consistently topped the Welsh League and supplied many of the international team. For a while Kevin did not get the recognition he deserved having fallen foul of the Wales coach Ron Waldron early in his rugby career after getting his marching orders in a Welsh Youth trial match when Waldron was in charge.

In 1987 Kevin took up an invitation via teammate John Perkins's family to spend the summer in New Zealand playing for the Bay of Plenty. He found it a hugely rewarding experience especially when they lined up against the Australians. The following year this all paid off when he returned with the full Wales team and gained the first of his nine caps against the All Blacks at Eden Park, Auckland. The Welsh were clobbered to the tune of 54-9 but a reporter complimented him by stating that 'Moseley on debut had shown real aggression'.

In 1989–90 he had gained further caps against Scotland, Ireland and Rumania and had by then accumulated well over 200 matches for Pontypool and captained the club. Unfortunately Prosser and most of his tough old hombres had long since retired and Pooler, although still powerful, was never to regain the stature it had enjoyed in the mid-1980s.

In early 1991 he suffered a personal disaster when he was ordered off for allegedly stamping on a French forward and was promptly handed a savage thirty-two week suspension by the powers that be. International rugby matches in those days were invariably pretty brutal – especially when France were in town – and Moseley was certainly no angel, but such a sentence would be laughed out of court in today's more legally transparent environment. To this day Kevin swears he was innocent of the particular incident in question.

He came back and was restored to the Wales team for the 1991 World Cup appearing against the Wallabies in Cardiff but matters were soon to take another turn. Kevin worked in the magazine printing industry and getting time off in those amateur days was never easy. A particularly unsympathetic response to his wishing to miss a routine midweek match for work reasons led to him leaving Pontypool and going down the road to Newport.

He had almost retired over the incident but he savoured his three seasons with Newport where he felt he played some of the best rugby of his entire career. In 1995 rugby turned professional and Kevin, although by then in his early thirties, was clearly going to be in demand. He nearly signed for Sale but opted to join ex-Pontypool colleague Mark Ring at West Hartlepool. At the time they were a premiership club but were soon relegated and have subsequently sunk virtually without trace.

Kevin had known Cornwall since childhood as he had stayed frequently with an aunt in Newquay and so, when Ring moved down to coach the Pirates, he also decided to come to Penzance. The club were then still down in South West I but had already signed some talented Welsh players including Steve Evans, Lee Mruk, Martyn Madden and Gerald Cordle.

Kevin joined in the dual role of player and as a forwards coach. Ring had been a hugely talented player but failed as a manager and was superseded by Peter Johnson with Kevin as his player-cum-assistant coach. He threw himself into the local rugby scene and even played for Cornwall in their title-winning team of 1999 – appearing in the Twickenham final despite nursing a broken hand.

That connection with the Cornwall team probably helped the Pirates to lure even more leading local players to the Mennaye and these now included Richard Carroll, Andy Birkett and that human dynamo that was Kevin Penrose. On the field he was a big man with an even bigger reputation and he had to endure a number of West Country self-styled 'hard nuts' hoping to make a name for themselves but generally did so with commendable restraint.

After a couple of years in the job, Johnson decided to move to London and Kevin was appointed Head Coach and immediately decided to give up playing. The club were in National III South and in the middle of a frustrating three season sequence of missing out narrowly on promotion. His first nine matches in charge were all won easily but the team then lost against Launceston and Blackheath followed by further reverses at Redruth and Plymouth and promotion ebbed away.

He finally led the club out of that division at Westcombe Park in April 2002 and followed it with the National II title a year later. Life in National I proved to be much harder with the demands greater and the pressures immense. He had acquired the coaching qualifications, had a small but dedicated squad and shown loyalty to the men who had gained promotion. However, a lack of bulky experienced forwards and a reliable goal-kicker threatened to embroil him in a relegation dog fight.

The squad was strengthened after Christmas and relegation fought off successfully but expectations and the resultant pressure now became even more intense. The following season the club made a hesitant start, recorded a plucky win over Exeter but then slumped to an embarrassing reverse at Sedgeley Park in early October 2004. A few days later Kevin lost his job.

He had by then gained a qualification in education and had already done some teaching at Truro and Helston. He had also developed an interest in sports psychology and soon landed the position of heading the Sports Academy at Bodmin College – a role he was to perform for the next ten years. During that time he also had a spell coaching Newquay Hornets.

He has now started up a company near Bodmin called 'Largavida Health Care' which specialises in health screening and developing dietary and exercise regimens for its clients as he continues to enjoy his life in Cornwall.

# Chris Stirling

Position: High Performance Manager
Date of Birth: 1962
Playing Career: Tawa RFC, Wellington B

Did you know? One early job Chris undertook was collecting corpses and transferring them to the local morgue.

In the summer of 2009 Chris Stirling arrived in Penzance in a new position of High Performance Manager and immediately set about changing the culture, values, fitness levels, performance analysis and general professionalism of the entire organisation. That he was to be spectacularly successful cannot be in doubt given a B & I Cup win, a playoff place in each of his three seasons and twice reaching the Championship finals.

A New Zealander, he was born and raised in rugby-mad Wellington. He began at the age of only four with his local club Tawa where he spent his entire playing career. Starting at hooker, he transferred to the backs as he worked up through the age and weight categories and was in his Tawa Secondary School team for four seasons. His main position was as a speedy, goal-kicking full-back although, having recorded eleven seconds for the 100 metres, he also appeared in the centre. In all he made 250 appearances for Tawa and featured in the Wellington B team. He also took part in cricket and running half-marathons.

Rugby was still totally amateur and Chris worked in the marketing side of the motor trade for twenty years being employed by the former All Black legend Murray Mexted. In 1995 he began coaching at Tawa and got such a taste for it that he left the world of cars and trucks to set out on a full-time rugby management career.

His first post took him to the Buller region – a remote area on the western coast of South Island. He moved his family to Westport and was based at the White Star Old Boys rugby club. Buller had always been the poor relations in terms of regional rugby but, during his three year stewardship, they reached the semi-finals of their regional championship for the first time ever.

He returned to Wellington to coach the Wainuiomata club where he had the opportunity to plan the development of coaches as well as players. After a year the club gained promotion having languished in the second tier for a quarter of a century. Moving back to coach his old club Tawa to win the Hardham Cup, he also coached the Wellington B, Colts and Academy teams which brought him into contact with two boys from Upper Hutt – Blair Cowan and Jonny Bentley.

He wanted to experience a taste of life outside New Zealand and jumped at an opportunity to come to England for a few weeks. The Pirates had been interested in a back-rower named Ati Olive and were put in contact with Chris to discover more about him. A further conversation developed with Dicky Evans who indicated that the Pirates had struggled with the new experimental laws and, given that they had already been tried in New Zealand, asked if he knew someone who might help. Chris immediately volunteered himself and in October 2008 came to Cornwall for a visit.

Once there, he observed everything and quickly ascertained that the club had great potential, enthusiastic coaches, some talented rugby players, wonderful volunteers and supporters plus a committed owner but lacked overall cohesion and direction. He was asked if he might come to Penzance on a longer term basis but, although personally keen and his family supportive, the issue was obtaining the appropriate visa and work permits. Fortunately his wife's English based family connections were enough to do the trick.

He arrived in the summer of 2009 plus his two new coaches Harvey Biljon and Ian Davies. Neither of them had known Chris previously but they quickly formed a strong triumvirate and began to lay the foundations for the next three years. He set about establishing a set of basic principles, got the players to understand more about the club and the people they represented and then embarked upon the toughest pre-season fitness programme any of the team had ever encountered. He established a players' room and insisted that everyone got smartened up for match days. The tee shirts and flip-flops disappeared and club blazers and ties suddenly made a miraculous return. Immediately the team looked prouder, bigger, taller, fitter and with an infinitely better focus on the job-in-hand.

The team were still playing at Camborne and, after thrashing Cardiff, went to the Harlequins for a tough pre-season friendly. The Quins put out a strong team including Robshaw, Monye, Easter and Care but had just been rocked by the 'bloodgate' scandal and nobody quite knew what to expect. On a scorching afternoon the Quins pulled away in the second half but not before the Pirates had shown a level of organisation and zest which boded well for the season ahead.

Perhaps as a reaction to their heavy training schedule or maybe through sheer bad luck, the team began with such a spate of injuries that Biljon was nominated as a bench replacement for the opener at Nottingham. The initial big 'find' was Bentley whom Chris had prised away from Japan although soon the talents of Cowan, the returning skipper Gavin Cattle, Dave Ward and Rob Cook all began to shine alongside him.

Having won the opening four matches, the team lost at Plymouth and a short run of defeats followed. The side really came through on Boxing Day when Albion were thrashed in the return at Camborne. From that point onwards the Pirates were going to be among the Championship front runners – notwithstanding the fact that they did not possess the stadium or facilities to capitalise on any league success by promotion to the Premiership.

This problem continued to cast a shadow over the club throughout his tenure in Cornwall and continues to do so today. Nevertheless the inaugural B & I Cup did not have stadium requirements and, following the destruction of Newport and Doncaster, the Pirates thrilled a packed Camborne by overcoming a confident Munster team to claim the trophy. It was a sweet moment for Chris but this was only to be the beginning.

That summer the club had dramatically switched its home matches back to Penzance and the supporters rose even further in his estimation by getting together and sprucing up the rather battered old Mennaye Field in just a few short weeks. He had kept all his best players and further strengthened the team by signing Albion's captain Kyle Marriott and their star centre Matt Hopper plus the outstanding Phil Burgess.

News of happenings down in the far South West began to filter into the public consciousness and, after a dramatic win at Worcester, Sky television started to become a regular visitor at Pirates matches. The previous year the team had failed in the playoffs but now they won their group, disposed of London Welsh in a thrilling semi-final but fell short to Worcester in a fine two-legged final.

Chris knew his team could improve still further and was confident that his third year would bring its just reward. Planning permission was granted for a new stadium near Truro and several new players were added to the squad. Unfortunately Bentley did not recover properly from an operation and hence the side lost its little talisman. Furthermore some of the new signings failed to deliver on expectations and then, to cap it all, the county council dramatically refused to sanction any expenditure on the proposed stadium and promotion was effectively a 'dead duck' for at least another couple of years.

Chris had family commitments in New Zealand and did not lack opportunities back home. He had set his heart on dragging the Pirates up to the top table but now this chance had been cruelly snatched away. His three-year contract was coming to an end and so with a heavy heart he decided to go – leaving supporters in Cornwall feeling bereft. He had always been approachable, courteous and self-evidently cared deeply about what he was doing. In his first season he had been 'hands on' in the coaching of the squad but, as things developed, he increasingly let Davies and Biljon take this over. He also enhanced the medical and rehabilitation support for injured players.

Returning to New Zealand he accepted a senior position with the NZ Rugby Union identifying and creating development plans for promising young players to become the potential All Blacks of the future. However he missed the daily 'buzz' of being involved in a professional rugby club and so has become the High Performance Manager of the Hurricanes who are one of the very top teams in the southern hemisphere.

This in a way is a similar role to that which he held at the Pirates but obviously on a very much larger scale. He still retains a great affection for English rugby and the Pirates in particular and still harbours a long term ambition to lead a team in the Premiership.

# CHAPTER TWO

# THE PLAYERS

## Joe Beardshaw

Position: Lock
Height/Weight: 6'5", 17st 7lbs
Date of birth: 1976
Matches: 75 + 6
Tries: 4

**Did you know?** Joe once played mini rugby in the same team as Josh Lewsey and one of his Gresham's School contemporaries was film and TV actress Olivia Colman.

Joseph John Beardshaw was born in Norwich and lived nearby where his father had a boat business on the Norfolk Broads. His father and two uncles played rugby at North Walsham and Joe had his first introduction to the game by watching them and playing mini rugby there himself from the age of only three.

His secondary school, Notre Dame in Norwich, played very little rugby although one of his contemporaries was the one-time Pirate fly-half and later Plymouth Albion coach James Shanahan. Despite this, he progressed through the schools trials and got his England Under 16 cap thanks to his development at North Walsham. After his GCSEs he went on to Gresham's School which has, among others, produced the Youngs family of Leicester and England fame.

At Gresham's he was again capped for England at Under-18 level in a team that featured Joe Worsley and a future Pirates colleague Tom Barlow. Wasps scouts were watching the England lads and he joined Worsley in making his way there. It was the last season of rugby being nominally amateur and he had a taste of the 1st XV senior Wasps squad which included Nick Popplewell and Steve Bates still in that old, more relaxed, environment during a minor European tournament in Holland.

He decided to do a gap year travelling before going to university and, through Wasps connections, joined a club in the Taranaki region of New Zealand named Tukapa. He enjoyed his time there and was selected to represent Taranaki itself and these experiences contributed much to his rugby education. Returning to the UK he signed a retainer contract at Wasps and went to study Ergonomics at Loughborough University. During this time he continued to play for the Wasps and made his Premiership debut against Bath at the Queens Park Rangers ground and played in the winning team in the Middlesex Sevens plate.

He gained further recognition by playing for the England Students and winning his first Under 21 cap on the England tour to Australia and then gaining a further six caps in the following Under 21 international campaign. That team included Jonny Wilkinson, Lewis Moody, Joe Worsley and Josh Lewsey.

In all he took part in approximately eighty Wasps first team matches over seven years which might have been more if he hadn't sustained a back injury. While never staying in the team for any extended run, he took part in many big matches in the Heineken Cup, the Tetley Bitter Cup Final and even a tour to New Orleans. He also went out on loan to Bedford when they were still in the Premiership. With a year left on his contract the Wasps were prepared to release him. He nearly went to Grenoble but his agent – Dick Best – found him a place with Glasgow and he had two happy years at Hughenden especially when his wife came up to join him and they bought their first house together.

Scottish rugby was a bit disjointed at the time and at twenty-nine he was on the lookout for a new challenge. Best knew the Pirates' CEO David Jenkins and from this connection Joe was signed in time for the move to Kenwyn near Truro. He loved the Cornish lifestyle, the countryside and especially the supporters and made his debut in a pre-season match at Launceston when he both scored a try and broke a rib in the same match.

He slotted in seamlessly beside Will James and later Heino Senekal in what was a very powerful team at the time and which led the Championship for a period until coming a cropper against the Harlequins. As with most Pirates of that time, the EDF run and final stand out clearest in his memory – especially the breathless win in the driving sleet at Headingley. His biggest impression of the final itself how incredibly hot it was out on the pitch and the emotional euphoria after it was all over.

In the two and a half seasons he was active in Cornwall he rarely missed a match. Sadly all that came to a sickening halt when his leg was locked as he was hit in a tackle against the Cornish All Blacks and a snapped ligament essentially finished his rugby career.

Joe was a big favourite with supporters as he was the core unit of a very solid set of forwards. He rarely did anything flashy but could always be relied upon to give his all in any situation. Regardless of the opposition, the weather or the score, big Joe was always right in the thick of it and possessed great stamina and physical strength.

Joe's influence on those around him could perhaps be typified by a probably long-forgotten situation in a rearranged night match at Bedford just before the EDF final. The Pirates had rested most of their best players and were getting a terrible pasting both up front and on the scoreboard itself. The match was already clearly lost when Joe came off the bench, rolled up his sleeves and suddenly everything tightened up as they took the initiative back from the hosts. A match which could have been lost by sixty points ended up by being only by thirty.

Since his enforced retirement from the game, Joe and his young family have returned to Norfolk where he works in the agricultural grain business. He has happily made a full recovery from his debilitating injury and keeps very fit by taking part in triathlons with the attendant cycling and swimming.

He even sneaked in a charity rugby match in Bahrain along the way.

# Joe Bearman

Position: Back Row
Height/Weight: 6'4", 16st 10lbs
Date of Birth: 1979
Matches: 138 + 22
Tries: 41

**Did you know?** Joe played mainly football at school and went for a trial with Everton.

Surely one of the very best forwards to emerge from Cornwall in recent years, Joe Bearman from Newquay was something of a teenage prodigy as the Pirates clawed their way up through the leagues and one who just got better and better.

Growing up in Newquay, he attended Tretherras School where he showed early promise as a footballer and played for Cornwall Schools as a striker. He began rugby when he was about fourteen and within a couple of years was playing for Cornwall Colts. Although this was in his familiar position in the back-row he had also turned out on the wing, centre and even at full-back as he continued to learn the game.

On leaving school in 1997 he began qualifying for the building trade at Cornwall Technical College and meanwhile played a handful of games for Newquay Hornets. He soon came to the notice of the ex-Wales centre Mark Ring who was briefly in charge of the Pirates and Joe joined the club on a YTS basis while continuing his studies at the Technical College. He made his debut off the bench in a friendly at Plymouth in a game in which Albion were very nearly toppled. Almost immediately Ring was replaced by Peter Johnson but, before the season ended, Joe had made his first start on the flank at Torquay. Nevertheless Johnson nurtured him carefully but, by the start of his third season, the now nineteen-year-old Joe was ready for regular inclusion.

The Millennium found the Pirates struggling to get up from National III South but, as the new century dawned, Joe established himself as a permanent fixture in the team. He was still only twenty but was making appearances not only in his favoured position in the back-row, but also at lock and occasionally in the backs playing both on the wing and in the centre. Promotion was narrowly missed, both in that season and the following one, but he had meanwhile made his bow for Cornwall against Surrey at Esher marking his debut with a try. However he missed out on the Cornwall Cup victory over Launceston and actually never took part in a county cup win.

It was equally unfortunate that a dispute between club and county over the vexed question of insuring professional players caused a protracted 'family feud' between them. This effectively excluded Joe and many of his contemporaries from representing Cornwall and everyone seemed to lose out in the process.

The Pirates then secured two promotions in successive seasons. Joe picked up a shoulder injury during a spiteful match in a hailstorm against the Old Patesians in early March and thus missed the Pirates' final victory at Westcombe Park to finally escape from National Division III. However season 2002/03 saw him emerge as one of the outstanding forwards in National II as the Pirates clinched the title against Stourbridge with several matches still to play. A rare defeat arising from a poor performance at Henley in mid-season had resulted in Joe taking over the captaincy from Nat Saumi and he held the position with only one short break for the rest of his time in Cornwall.

Thus when the Pirates made their first appearance in National I (now the Championship), it was Joe who proudly led them out to face a newly-relegated Bristol at the Memorial Ground. That season was a considerable challenge as the entire club fought to come to terms with the far greater professionalism and physicality with which they had now to contend every week. He began the season with Richard Carroll, Lakalaka Waquanivere and Kevin Penrose as his colleagues in the back-row but, by the following April, Joe was the only one to have retained his place.

In the summer the captaincy passed initially to Martin Morgan and subsequently to the charismatic Lodewyk Hattingh. That second season proved to be far more successful as the Pirates had at last found their feet and he now was teamed up with Hattingh, Iva Motusaga and Tim Cowley and as such was then the only England-qualified player in the back row.

Poor Hattingh suffered a severe career-ending head injury just as the new season kicked off and Joe was restored to lead the team. That summer they had been rebranded as the Cornish Pirates and had decamped to Kenwyn near Truro. By then he was the subject of continual interest from several Premiership clubs and in particular Sale Sharks. Jim McKay had assembled a strong team but, with Harlequins having been sensationally relegated the previous year, there was only ever likely to be one winner when the final league table was to be published. As the season neared its end, Joe decided to move not to Sale but rather closer to home with the Gwent Dragons and moved to live in Cardiff where he has remained ever since. Initially he shared accommodation with fellow Pirate Matt Jess who had also signed for the Dragons at the same time.

The Dragons had some top performers in the back-row including the British Lions Number 8 Michael Owen. Joe played his way into the team as a flanker and soon established himself as a regular squad member both in the Magners League and in Europe. He had never played for any England representative teams and thus, after three years residing in Wales, he was technically eligible to turn out for Wales. He was duly called up into the squad but then suffered a nagging groin injury which refused to clear up and his rugby was severely curtailed for eighteen months and his chance of a cap receded once more.

In all he made seventy-seven competitive first team appearances for the Dragons over five years but would undoubtedly have taken that number past the century mark had it not been for his injury. In 2011 it was time to move on and, having considered offers from Bristol and Stade Français, he opted to join the Ospreys and went straight into the team.

He and his Cornish wife were settled happily in Cardiff and the move merely entailed him going a little way in the opposite direction along the M4. The Ospreys had generally done better than the Dragons over the previous few years and, at the time of writing, Joe has made around ninety first team appearances for them and has a host of fond memories of many Heineken Cup and other European cup ties – especially those fought out in France.

He has done some coaching with a local Cardiff club named Old Illtydians and also with the Cardiff Under 18s having gained his Level Two badge. His future ambitions however lie more in the area of utilising his building skills and venturing into property development.

Although now thirty-six, he has a one year extension on his contract and has no plans to finish playing yet. He still goes back to Cornwall frequently to see family and friends, plays golf and has naturally been working away on his house in Cardiff.

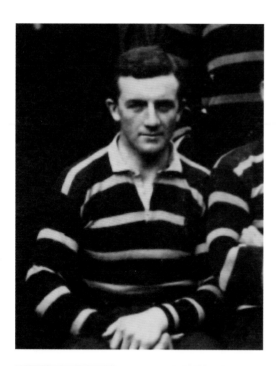

# Barrie Bennetts

Position: Wing / Centre
Height/Weight: 5' 8", 11st 0lbs
Date of Birth: 1883
Date of Death: 1958
Matches: Not known
Tries: Not known

Did you know? Aside from all his sporting activities Barrie starred in a stage production of *Liberty Hall* at Penzance Pavilion in 1912.

When your parents have saddled you with a name like Barzillai Beckerleg Bennetts it must be a relief to go through life with everyone just calling you 'Barrie'. He was born in Penzance as the son of J. H. Bennetts the founder of the eponymous family coal business which has supplied West Penwith for well over a century. However, having attended Bridgend College, he trained for the legal profession.

He was clearly a man of enormous energy who seemed to excel in a bewildering variety of sports and other activities although it was rugby which brought him to real prominence. Rugby players today can only concentrate upon one sport but Barrie also represented Cornwall at cricket, hockey and golf. He was also a top tennis player who would undoubtedly have represented the Duchy in that sport as well had Cornwall actually had a county team at the time. Furthermore he played for Penzance Football Club in four Cornwall Cup finals and was by all accounts a very accomplished performer at the billiards table.

Records of Penzance matches are hard to come by apart from some old minute books and occasional newspaper reports, but it is known that he was in the Penzance team as early as 1901–02 playing either as a centre or on the wing. He was a slightly-built man but was exceptionally quick with a bewildering swerve and sidestep.

While studying law in London, Barrie turned out for Richmond and also played for both Redruth and Devonport Albion. He made his debut for Cornwall on the wing at Bristol against Gloucestershire and went on to play some forty-two times for his county. That team at Bristol was captained by Dr R. C. Lawry whose widow, Mavis Lawry, would one day become the Pirates' first president upon her husband's premature death.

In 1905 he was on the wing when the first ever All Blacks came to Camborne but Barrie was unable to do much about it as they ran in eleven unanswered tries. His opposite number was a man named Bunny Abbott who was then considered to be the finest winger in the world. The following year at Redruth it was much closer when he lined up against the Springboks outside Redruth's brilliant Bert Solomon and the Cornish only lost by 3-9.

All Cornwall rugby fans can recite two key dates – 1991 and 1908. That Edwardian Cornwall team had a brilliant set of backs, five of whom were either already Internationals or would become so in the near future – including Barrie. Despite a try from Barrie, Devon won in Plymouth and thus Cornwall had to battle through a triangular playoff to win the South West Group and proceed to a semi-final with Middlesex followed by the historic Final with Durham. The story of that match has been retold many times with Cornwall triumphant but suffice it to say that Barrie was sent flashing in for the final try from a perfectly-timed pass from Solomon.

By this time his reputation had spread far and wide and he was invited onto the Barbarians Easter tour of South Wales and played against Penarth and Cardiff. The following season Cornwall twice played the Australian Wallabies. The first was at Camborne and Barrie took his customary place on the wing but the second held a more historic significance. As County Champions, the men from Cornwall were invited to play the Wallabies again in a special match to close the Olympic Games at the White City. Unfortunately Barrie had to withdraw unwell on the morning of the match and was replaced by Bert Solomon's brother Barney. The game turned out to be a bit of a 'damp squib' as Cornwall lost heavily in a thick London fog in front of a sparse crowd. Perhaps it was not such a bad game to miss.

This was borne out by the fact that just a few weeks later he made his England debut against those same Wallabies at Blackheath. England went down but he soon got his second cap against Wales at Cardiff Arms Park. This time he was in familiar company as one of four Cornishmen in the team and found himself lining up outside Tommy Wedge and Maffer Davey with John Jackett behind him at full-back. Unfortunately England went down again and Barrie's England career was over.

County rugby, however, was still very much on the agenda. Cornwall overcame the Midlands at Redruth by 26-8 during which Barrie scored two superb tries to renew acquaintance with Durham in a second Final at West Hartlepool. All of Cornwall's famous backs were on show but the pack had been weakened and Durham took their revenge with Barrie reportedly never getting a pass. He then went on a second Easter Barbarians tour facing the same opponents.

In 1910 a British Isles team was sent out to South Africa but the Argentinians also felt they should invite a 'British Isles' team too. The sport in Argentina was already hugely popular and it was resolved that a good team should be sent. In truth, this tour hardly qualifies the participants to be considered as 'British Lions' but under the influential Major R. V. Stanley they had a great tour and Barrie played in the centre in two more 'internationals' in Buenos Aires.

By now he was established in Penzance at a firm of solicitors soon to be called Boase & Bennetts and taking an increasingly prominent role in the town's affairs. He continued to play with both Penzance and Cornwall for another couple of seasons appearing against the touring Springboks for a second time in October 1912.

With the coming of the First World War he served as an officer in the Argyll and Sutherland Highlanders and saw action in France where he was mentioned in despatches. Amazingly his military career was not to end with the Armistice as he was one of the very first men in Penzance to volunteer for the Home Guard in 1940 when he was by then aged fifty-seven.

Away from sport his range of interests was staggering. He worked tirelessly for the RNLI and in particular the Penlee Lifeboat and in 1949 received the MBE not for his sporting prowess but for his service to the Penzance community. In addition he was the county coroner, was President of Penzance cricket club, a talented stage actor and, as a fine viola player, was a moving spirit in the establishment of the Penzance Orchestral Society. Barrie was a lifetime bachelor which is probably just as well as any poor wife would probably never have seen him!

When the Penzance and Newlyn clubs joined forces in 1945 he played his role in bringing this to fruition and of course it was Barrie, as the elder statesman, who performed the ceremonial kick-off at the inaugural match with Guy's Hospital.

In later life, he was President of Cornwall Rugby Union from 1945–50 and continued to work tirelessly for the RNLI getting a Lifetime Governorship from the Duke of Kent in 1957. The following year he died at his brother's house in his beloved Penzance.

# Jonny Bentley

Position: Fly Half
Height/Weight: 5' 7", 12st 13lbs
Date of Birth: 1986
Matches: 65 + 1
Tries: 17

Did you know? Jonny and Blair Cowan grew up and played rugby together from when they were both five years old.

New Zealander Jonathan Bentley was born and raised in Upper Hutt – a town a few miles from Wellington.

He started getting interested in rugby watching his elder brother play and, being eight years younger, generally got the job of ball boy. His brother was apparently a very promising player but suffered badly from injuries. Their father did not play but Jonny's maternal grandfather had once been to the UK to play Rugby League for Widnes.

Beginning in the Upper Hutt Under 6s, he worked his way up through the age groups and then he and his friend Blair Cowan moved on together to St Patrick's senior school which already had 'Thomas the Tank' (Exeter's Tom Waldrom) as a pupil. He played a bit of cricket as a wicketkeeper and did well as an 800-metre runner but rugby was always his enduring passion. Jonny played for the various age groups representing Wellington whose area teams took on all the major provinces such as Auckland and Waikato. Those junior Wellington teams were coached by Chris Stirling.

Jonny played club rugby with the Wellington Lions for a couple of years but felt he was losing out repeatedly due to his perceived lack of size. As with many New Zealanders, he also cherished a strong desire to travel and wanted the chance to play rugby professionally while doing so. One of his other Wellington coaches was Earl Eva'a, a Samoan who had just been appointed to a club in Japan.

So it came about that he signed up for a team called Yokogawa All Stars which was based around a company of that name in the western suburbs of Tokyo. They had just been promoted to the Japanese First Division but, with a smallish pack, they were generally on the back foot which made any fly-half's job especially difficult. Furthermore he found the language barrier a big problem and after a year was ready to move on again.

He was looking to Chris Stirling for a reference regarding a possible move to England with Birmingham & Solihull Bees but, with his old friend Blair Cowan already installed in Cornwall, it was not hard for the newly-appointed Stirling to point him towards Camborne. Once installed, he was soon making everyone sit up and take notice.

He seemed to ooze class from the moment he first stepped onto the pitch against Cardiff and then he got a try and showed up well in defence against a very strong Harlequins team at The Stoop. Possessed of a bewildering sidestep aligned to blistering pace over that vital first ten yards and carrying the ball in both hands, he quickly established himself as a star in the Championship. Whenever he made one of his darting breaks Pirates fans would literally jump off their seats in anticipation. Soon however a long-standing adductor muscle problem saw him reluctantly passing his goal-kicking duties onto first Rhys Jones and then, almost providentially, to the metronomic Rob Cook.

He played the first four matches and the Pirates won them all to stand briefly at the top of the Championship. That muscle injury then flared up and he was out for a few weeks and the unbeaten record immediately disappeared at Plymouth on the first week he was absent. He was back by mid-November and proceeded to give a long string of exciting displays especially on Boxing Day when Plymouth Albion were thrashed in ample revenge for their earlier win at Brickfields.

That first season ended with the B & I Cup triumph in the final over Munster and by then Jonny realised he had joined a very successful and moreover happy ship. He had struck up a great partnership with his captain Gavin Cattle whom he admired as an outstanding leader and one who had established a very good rapport with referees which Jonny felt helped the Pirates' cause enormously.

The next season (2010/11) was probably the best and happiest in Jonny's entire rugby career to date. Coach Harvey Biljon had raised the skill levels of all the backs by constant practice and by then Jonny had the aggressive and spectacular Matt Hopper signed to play alongside him. That year the Pirates opposed the ultimate champions Worcester no less than five times and in almost every one the two young Pirates repeatedly ripped through their much fancied opponents. In the second leg of the Championship Final the Sky TV panellists were unanimous in rating Jonny above the celebrated Andy Goode who was his opposite number for the Warriors. This was no fluke as Jonny had already done precisely the same thing on two previous occasions during the season.

Despite all the euphoria a problem was lurking and required to be resolved immediately. Jonny's adductor and groin muscle problems had been 'managed' for months but by then a complicated operation was required. This was only partially successful and it was not until late October that he returned to face London Welsh at Old Deer Park. Normal service appeared to be resumed when he scored a neat try and generally steered the Pirates to an exciting draw but disaster struck the following week at Brickfields when he was led off again after only twenty minutes. It looked bad but nobody in their worst nightmares could have imagined he would only ever play one more match for the Pirates.

However hard he tried, his rehabilitation received one setback after another including tearing his Achilles tendon in a freak training ground accident. In all he was trying to return to fitness throughout the rest of that season and the whole of the following one. It was incredibly frustrating for his horde of Pirates fans but doubly so for Jonny who just wanted to get out there and play rugby.

His departure to sign for Gloucester was inevitably a controversial one. He had at last appeared to have regained his fitness and the Premiership club, no doubt recalling his exploits a full eighteen months previously, wanted him initially as cover for the England hopeful Freddie Burns whom it was assumed would be away with the International squad for much of the season. The life of a professional rugby player is brutally short and Jonny felt he had to take the opportunity being presented. Furthermore hopes for the stadium at Truro were once again being dashed, Stirling had returned to New Zealand and several of his closest colleagues were themselves moving on – including his best buddy Blair Cowan. After much heart-searching he followed his colleagues Rob Cook and Drew Locke to Kingsholm. Most supporters understood his career dilemma and wished him well but a few just could not somehow quite bring themselves to forgive him.

Gloucester proved to be another disappointment. Firstly Burns was overlooked in favour of Owen Farrell and Jonny picked up yet more injuries including a damaged medial ligament. He got his one big opportunity in the seething cauldron of Thomond Park in Limerick against a rampant Munster. It was in the Heineken Cup and there could hardly be a tougher place to make a debut. He had hoped to retain his place but it was not to be and, apart from a couple of LV Cup games, he found himself languishing in the A team.

Towards the end of that season he had a short spell on loan with Leeds Carnegie and enjoyed the experience. They reached the semi-finals of the Championship only to be edged out by London Welsh and he then took part in his second B & I Cup Final – this time against Leinster.

His mentor from Cornwall, Harvey Biljon, had recently taken over in Jersey and so it was next stop the Channel Islands for the little Kiwi where he joined a host of other ex-Pirates including Locke. After two years in the Channel Islands he returned to New Zealand and to his old mates at Wellington Lions.

Jonny Bentley has come through some tough times and often had to play through the pain of injury. Despite his lack of inches, he was never once afraid to get stuck in and make his tackles against the biggest and lumpiest Championship forwards and could control a match and kick into space to keep his pack moving forwards with the best of them. But it was that dazzling sidestep, the drop of the shoulder and the blistering speed off the mark to cut through and either set up a try or surge over the line himself that Pirates fans will never, ever forget.

# Adrian Bick

Position: Flanker
Height/Weight: 5' 11", 14st 7lbs
Date of Birth: 1966
Matches: 277
Tries: 61

**Did you know?** Adrian is a crew member of the Penlee Lifeboat working with another ex-Pirate Patch Harvey and is also believed to be the only Cornishman to have played senior rugby in four different decades.

Everyone associates Adrian Bick with the great Cornwall teams of 1991 and 1992 celebrating at Twickenham in the famous Cornish tartan. Therefore it may surprise some that he was actually born in Hertford and only arrived in Penzance at the age of ten.

His father had played as a centre in the army and so, having enrolled at St Paul's School, he was soon down at the Pirates minis and juniors then under the eye of Phil Harvey. This continued when he moved on to Humphry Davy School where the games teachers John Matthews and Steve Ashall were both sometime Pirates who immediately recognised that Adrian had something special. He was inevitably picked for Cornwall at each age group and even went on a tour to Portugal.

He got his chance in the Pirates team over Easter in 1984 aged only sixteen and began the next season celebrating a hatful of tries against Concarneau – a fishing port in Brittany which is twinned with Penzance. He then went to Penwith College to do his A Levels and for the next two years rarely missed a game. Despite his youth he stood out like a beacon in a team which was often struggling against relatively modest opposition in front of only a handful of spectators.

He then went to train to be a teacher at St Paul's College in Cheltenham and his Pirate appearances were thus limited to when he was home on holiday. He had the galling experience of being selected to go with what was in essence the England Under 20 team to South Africa but, no doubt due to his moving between college and home, he never received his invitation letter until after the pre-tour training was under way and so he missed out. It was a bitter blow.

On a brighter note he represented both England and Great Britain Colleges and also the Combined England Students in the first student World Cup in France plus getting a game against the full Wallabies team at Oxford and only losing by 18-36.

He also made his debut for Cornwall in September 1987 against the South Wales Police at Bridgend. It was an eventful baptism as Cornwall's hooker Brian Andrew was ordered off and Adrian found himself completing the match in the middle of the front row. He retained his place for the rest of that season as well as the following one when Cornwall went down narrowly to Durham in the final at Twickenham.

One of his fellow students at St Paul's was the future England full-back Jon Callard and they both joined Newport for a brief spell. When Callard moved on to Bath, Adrian did likewise to join fellow Cornishmen Graham Dawe, Martin Haag and Barry Trevaskis. Once there he found his chances were limited by Andy Robinson who was then considered to be one of the best flankers in Europe. As a result he only had about a dozen senior games for Bath - one of which was against the Rumanian army team Steau Bucharest. Taken to the dressing room for treatment, he fell into conversation with the opposing captain who was also being stitched up. Just a year or so later the poor man was shot dead in the uprising against President Ceaucescu.

Adrian's luck was not great either for he then broke a leg and, having left college, took a job with a firm of insurance underwriters. For a while he played for Lydney but then came back to Cornwall and signed for Plymouth Albion while working at the Newlyn fish market. Albion then sat several levels above the Pirates and it was during this period that he played his major role in the great Cornwall exploits at Twickenham of 1991 and 1992.

His chief memory of the Yorkshire triumph was that, although the game lasted for nearly two hours, he was so pumped up with adrenalin and the incessant roar of the thousands of black and gold bedecked Cornish fans that he felt he could run for ever.

Soon after that match he was approached by Dicky Evans. It was still a year or two before Evans took any official position with the Pirates but he persuaded Adrian to come back to Penzance and to bring in some more players – the first being a lock from Australia named John Frize. The Pirates were then languishing in the Western Counties League opposing teams like Okehampton, Saltash and Old Culverhaysians but both he and Evans had far bigger plans.

He returned to teaching, taking a job at Penryn School where he has taught ever since. After a year he took over from Jamie Dean as club captain for the next three seasons. He was in his prime but rugby was still an amateur sport – very much so in Cornwall – and the Pirates stayed rooted in the Western Counties League. Nevertheless progress was being made, debts cleared and training improved. By the time the club celebrated its Golden Jubilee, in 1995, Evans was installed as President. Things then took off and Adrian was at the centre of it all.

Professionalism and two promotions followed swiftly and in 1998 he led the side to winning the South West I League and to taking their place in the National Leagues for the very first time. At the end of that year he had the great satisfaction of leading the Pirates to a victory over Launceston to win the Cornwall Cup for the first time since 1976.

He was there again the following year for a reprise of the Launceston final but he was now often in competition for the number seven shirt with another 'perpetual motion' man Kevin Penrose and the ex-Bristol and Coventry man Derek Eves.

When he returned from Plymouth Albion, Adrian had frequently played alongside his elder brother Julian, and he decided to rejoin him at St Just along with another ex-Pirate skipper Martin Murrish. He had a couple of years there as their player/coach and then came back to Penzance to join Mounts Bay during their own breakneck charge up through the league system. He also masterminded Bay's own Intermediate Cup Final success at

Twickenham within just a couple of hours of the Pirates having just done likewise at the level above.

He continued to coach Mounts Bay in their brief visit to National I but then sadly the money ran out and the club disbanded. He now combines his teaching at Penryn with working with ex-Mounts Bay colleague Ricky Pellow at the Exeter Academy.

# Phil Burgess

Position: Flanker
Height/Weight: 6' 1", 15st 0lbs
Date of Birth: 1988
Matches: 66 + 21
Tries: 29

Did you know? Phil is quite an accomplished pianist.

Philip James Burgess has his roots in Surrey. He was born in Frimley, grew up in nearby Camberley and his father had played rugby on the wing for Warlingham. Indeed this was a rugby playing family in which both his brother and sister also played for Camberley. The brother, who is now coaching at Richmond, once played junior rugby there with Phil's one-time Pirate colleague Rhodri McAtee.

Sport at Tomlinscote School in Frimley did not include rugby so Phil's athletic outlets were mainly football and orienteering with rugby confined to Camberley RFC at weekends. At this time he was a centre and as such was good enough to get into the Surrey schools team despite coming from a non-rugby playing state school.

As he entered the sixth form, two important developments came into his rugby life. He was invited to join the so-called Harlequins Academy and took the advice of a county schools selector to switch to the back row of the scrum. At that time the Harlequins Academy was limited to a series of holiday coaching camps at Aldershot rather than the more formal system in operation today. However, on the advice of a coach at Camberley named Alan Rise, he joined the London Welsh Colts who played at a much more competitive level in that they took part in a Welsh Youth league. This took Phil to places like Blackwood and Pontypool which was an education in itself.

On leaving school he deferred his entry to Loughborough for a year and joined the Harlequins as a contracted player. His experience was one that has been mirrored by many promising young players in recent years. He got lots of training but precious little game time as the Quins had a host of good flankers coming through – not least the future England captain Chris Robshaw. His only first team opportunity was a cameo appearance from the bench against Newcastle. Perhaps it was a sign towards the future that he represented the Quins in the Middlesex Sevens at Twickenham where his speed and ball handling skills more than outweighed his relative lack of bulk.

Although the Harlequins offered him an extension to his contract he resolved to take up the opportunity at Loughborough University where he read Sports Science and Geography. At the time he thought about going into teaching, the police or possibly joining the army but for the time being it was rugby all the way.

He was in the Loughborough team for all the three seasons he was at the university and was made captain for his final year. Loughborough has always had an outstanding reputation for producing elite sportsmen and women and the facilities and coaching are second to none. Phil obtained six caps for the England Students team and played in France and Portugal. He also took the opportunity to play more sevens which included the Safari tournament in East Africa.

As he came to the end of his time at university, Phil began looking for a suitable club and he was not short of options. One of his senior coaches was the ex-Wasps and Cornwall player Alan Buzza which helped make the initial connection but it was his meeting with Ian Davies which made a profound impression upon him. He knew nothing of Cornwall but came down to Camborne to watch the B & I Final with Munster. The place, the passionate crowd and the style of play all struck a chord and he soon signed on.

When he joined it was known that he could still operate in the backs if required but it was his pace, intelligence, tackling and ball handling that were the assets he brought to the team. By Championship standards he was rather on the small side for a back-row player but with men like McGlone, Cowan and Betty to provide the muscle, Phil could provide the music.

He celebrated his debut with a try against Doncaster and was regularly on the score sheet including a hat-trick against Moseley. Many of his tries came from exciting long distance bursts up field – none more so than one at Bristol in the play-offs at the end of his second season. All this got due recognition when he was selected for the Championship team against the Maoris.

He experienced numerous highlights during his time at Penzance including an outstanding performance in front of the television cameras in a home game with Worcester Warriors. This he repeated a couple of months later in the two-legged final against the same opponents. He marked his second final the following season with a try against London Welsh.

He had settled well in Cornwall and his partner Francesca also worked for the club as a video analyst. Despite this Premiership clubs inevitably came looking and there was interest from London Irish and Gloucester. Once again it was his speed and ball skills which were seen as his chief assets and so it was perfectly logical for professional sevens to be an attractive alternative.

The sevens circuit also provides a tremendous opportunity for a rugby player to see the world being very much a global sport with competitions held throughout the year in numerous countries rather like F1 motor racing. He was offered a two-year contract with the England Sevens team and this seemed to tick all the right boxes. Phil soon found himself playing in Australia, South Africa, Dubai, Las Vegas, Hong Kong, Japan, Russia and New Zealand and loved every minute of it. The highlight so far was the Commonwealth Games at Ibrox Park in Glasgow which had a brilliant atmosphere and just whetted his appetite even more so for the forthcoming Olympics in Rio de Janeiro.

Phil hopefully still has a number of years of rugby in front of him but his longer term ambition is to work in human resources (which is also Francesca's chosen career) or project management. No doubt he will.

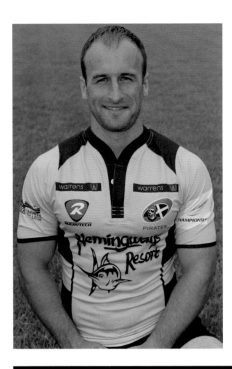

# Gavin Cattle

Position: Scrum Half
Height/Weight: 5' 9", 13st 0lbs
Date of Birth: 1980
Matches: 183 + 29
Tries: 40

Did you know? Gavin, together with Alan Paver and Tim Cowley, once undertook the most dangerous bike ride in the world down a mountainside near La Paz in Bolivia.

Gavin Cattle was born in Bridgend but brought up in the village of Pencoed a few miles outside the town. As with many proud Welshmen, his father was something of a rugby fanatic who had played for Maesteg, Pencoed and Bridgend but during Gavin's childhood was by then with the local club Ogmore Vale.

He began rugby with the mini section of the Vale club. Thanks both to his father and a family friend named Malcolm Witts, Gavin was encouraged to pursue his rugby and in due course transferred to Pencoed where he progressed through the age groups. Already settled as a scrum-half, he showed sufficient promise to be drafted into the Wales Under 18 squad but found the future International Dwayne Peel blocking his way to a coveted cap.

He was keen on sport generally and enjoyed football on the left wing with javelin throwing in the summer and so went off to Wolverhampton University to study for a degree in Sport and Leisure. At about that time he suffered a fractured vertebra in his spine and was actually advised to give up rugby but thankfully this proved unduly pessimistic and he was soon able to resume playing.

While at university he often returned to Pencoed where, as a bouncy young prospect, he experienced some of the roughest treatment of his entire career. He was also selected for the Wales Under 21 and Student Exiles teams. He had a short spell with Worcester Warriors in their Development Squad and then signed for Birmingham & Solihull in 2000. They were then a solid National I side with aspirations towards a better stadium and higher things.

After a productive three seasons during which he featured in around eighty matches, he signed for Orrell who were then constructing a strong team to challenge for a return to the

Premiership. They were coached by Jim McKay and included not only future England man Nick Easter but Wade Kelly, Richard Welding and Peter Ince who would all soon become fellow Pirates. The newly-promoted Pirates were thrashed twice by a Cattle-inspired Orrell team which missed out narrowly on promotion. At that point the Wigan RL owner David Whelan lost all interest in rugby union and cynically pulled all his money out leaving the club abandoned and broke.

Gavin, McKay and several others moved to Rotherham but, just before a pre-season friendly, the Titans also lost their backers and effectively went bankrupt. Gavin must have felt his career was cursed. Fortunately at this point Dicky Evans stepped in and McKay, Gavin, Kelly and Ince all came to Cornwall.

He made his debut coincidentally back at Birmingham & Solihull and quickly established himself ahead of the experienced Ricky Pellow and Rhodri McAtee who was soon moved to the wing. In January superb performances at Exeter and Bristol cemented his place, probably positioned him as a future leader and within a year he was taking over as captain from Joe Bearman. Over the next three seasons the Pirates never dropped out of the top four places and their inspiring skipper hardly missed a match.

For the first two years he had been linked with alternately fellow Welshman Lee Jarvis and the equally talented Tom Barlow. In 2006 the Pirates brought in the cool Argentinian/ Italian Alberto di Bernardo and he and Gavin seemed made for one another. The climax was undoubtedly the EDF final at Twickenham and it was Gavin's honour to lift the trophy and bring it home to be paraded through the welcoming streets of Penzance.

Almost inevitably the big clubs took a close interest and he decided to go back to Wales to join Llanelli Scarlets whose scrum-half, the self-same Dwayne Peel, was expected to be on constant World Cup and Six Nations duty for Wales. It proved to be something of a disappointment. Even though he managed about thirty Magners League and European appearances over the next two seasons – he missed Cornwall and regular game time.

A new Pirates coaching team was just arriving and, within a few weeks of pre-season training, Chris Stirling had decided who his captain was going to be. It proved to be one of many sound decisions he was to make during his tenure.

The Pirates had dipped slightly during his absence but Gavin now found himself in an enthusiastic new regime and the positive results soon began to flow. Over the next three years the Pirates lifted the inaugural B & I Cup, and then reached two Championship finals – five huge matches and Gavin led the team in every one of them. Perhaps his greatest game was the semi-final against London Welsh when he virtually won the match with one of his characteristic sniping breaks for a try in front of his adoring fans on the Newlyn terrace.

By now he was settled happily back in Cornwall and starting a young family near Truro where he had begun to do some part-time coaching. As a senior professional he was also helping to develop the younger scrum-halves that had joined the club – in particular James Doherty and Tom Kessell.

He was widely acknowledged to be the most consistently effective scrum-half in the Championship and was selected in the Rugby Paper's 'Dream Team' for four consecutive years. He featured in the Championship team against the New Zealand Māoris at Doncaster in 2012 and in the autumn of 2014 he played for the Barbarians against the Combined Services at Bath.

When Harvey Biljon left to manage Jersey RFC Ian Davies needed an experienced man to help mould the young recruits coming into the club. Although still willing and able to play Gavin was the obvious choice right on his doorstep.

The transition from being a player to a player-coach is inevitably a big change – not least in the working hours involved. However, with Kessell by then clearly ready for a regular Championship starting place, Gavin was able to devote more time to planning and coaching while keeping sufficiently fit to be called upon to play if required.

# Rob Cook

Position: Full Back
Height/Weight: 6' 0", 14st 7lbs
Date of Birth: 1984
Matches: 100 + 4
Tries: 24

**Did you know?** Rob played football as a junior for Lincoln City and cricket for both Leicestershire and Lincolnshire.

All round sportsman Rob Cook came from a sports-minded family in which his father had played semi-professional football with Boston United. He was born in Lincoln and first came to prominence with the round ball while at North Kesteven Comprehensive and attracted the attention of scouts from Lincoln City. He signed for them and played for their junior teams as a striker and occasional old-fashioned wingman.

He soon began to show even more promise as a cricketer and it was for the summer game that he followed his brother who had just gained a sports scholarship to Oakham School in Rutland. Cricket continued to be his main interest and he signed for Leicestershire turning out as a batsman and wicketkeeper for their Second XI on a number of occasions.

However rugby now came along to beckon Rob. The Oakham staff included the inspirational ex-Leicester flanker Ian 'Dosser' Smith (who reputedly earned his nickname at school due to his habit of falling asleep in class) and it was he as much as anyone who lit the spark in Rob for all that would come later.

Having left school, Rob took a gap year playing and coaching cricket in Sydney where his eyes were opened to sport being played at a much more intense level. Returning to England in 2002, he went to Worcester University where he took a degree in Sports Science. His personal tug-of-war between cricket and rugby began to intensify and he found himself in due course playing at fly-half for the English Universities team for which he gained four caps.

Upon graduation he joined another Worcester man named Paul Westgate in signing for Nuneaton RFC who were then in National Division II and coached by the ex-Rotherham star Mike Umaga. Unfortunately, although Rob did well enough dividing his time between full-back and fly-half and being named Player of the Year, the Nuns were immediately relegated. However they bounced back with a vengeance the following season during which his fourteen tries and general play saw him selected for the England Counties team who were then coached by Harvey Biljon.

The South African saw much to admire in Rob's talent and approach and it was no surprise that he followed Biljon into full-time professional rugby. What was slightly more surprising was that it was to be with the Cornish Pirates. The expectation had been that Biljon would be going to Bristol but by the time Rob received the not unexpected call, it was not from the banks of the Severn but from miles away in West Cornwall. Rob liked what he heard but, apart from a few days holiday in Newquay, had never been near the place in his life.

There was the added complication that he had a second income as captain of his home county Lincolnshire in the Minor Counties cricket league. However, having succeeded in landing an initial two year contract, he put pen to paper and Bristol's loss was very much the Pirates' gain.

Having joined Chris Stirling's exciting Pirates squad in 2009, he took a few weeks to break into the team. He played his first match at full-back in a pre-season friendly against Cardiff at Camborne and made a solid early impression in a runaway victory. However, he did not make the starting line-up for the early fixtures but came off the bench against Moseley.

In early October he made his full debut at Plymouth starting on the wing and then was soon tried as a fly-half replacement for the injured Bentley. A week later he was switched by Stirling to full-back against Bristol and within another fortnight had taken over the goal-kicking from the injured Jimmy Moore. These were the two situations in which he soon reigned supreme for the following three years.

To begin with he continued to cover at fly-half for Bentley with Lancastrian Wes Davies holding down the full-back berth. However, when the Pirates played their first B & I Cup match against a scratch Scottish team called Gael Force he took over not only the full-back shirt but the kicking duties as well. A thrilling last minute touchline conversion at Moseley to win the game with the final kick of the match was soon followed by an outstanding performance on a frozen pitch at Coventry where he scored a brilliant 70-yard counter-attacking try which nailed down his place for keeps.

An untimely hand injury received from a nasty tip tackle at Bedford led to him missing the B & I final victory over Munster at the end of his first season but, having had the summer to recover, he became a virtual ever-present for the rest of his time in Cornwall.

That summer he signed to play cricket for St Just and enjoyed two summers playing for that very successful Cornish League team. His Pirate sponsors were the local sports-loving hoteliers Peter George and his wife Anita who were avid supporters of both St Just cricket and the Cornish Pirates and so it all fitted together very well for all concerned.

The following season saw the Pirates reach the Championship Finals playoffs against Worcester. It was at Sixways that Worcester had lost their only game of the season when they fell to a last minute 40-yard penalty from Rob who defied a screeching crowd by nervelessly slotting the winner. At the end of the season he bravely turned out for the second leg of the final back at Sixways despite the knowledge that his father was gravely ill.

During his final season he repeatedly demonstrated his cricketer's hands under the high ball, his counter-attacking running and an effective kick-and-chase tactic all coupled with deadly accurate, if slightly idiosyncratic, goal kicking. This was later described by TV pundit Austin Healey as resembling a constipated llama. Regardless of that he reached a remarkable 1,000 points in all games over a mere three years which included a fine haul of twenty-three tries.

That season had many highlights including a thrilling demolition of Bristol in the first leg of the Championship semi-finals when he gave possibly his most assured display to register a personal tally of twenty-five points during a remarkable 45-24 victory on Sky television. A further fine performance kept the Pirates' noses in front and so Rob's last matches were in the two-legged finals with London Welsh.

Inevitably a few Premiership clubs came knocking and, having rejected an offer from Sale Sharks, he eventually signed for Nigel Davies at Gloucester. He did so alongside two other Pirate backs in Bentley and the elusive centre Drew Locke. None of them made the Premiership team to begin with and on one occasion Rob came back to guest for the Pirates and land the telling penalty kick to beat Plymouth Albion.

However, after a few weeks he got his big chance against the Wasps for the injured Olly Morgan and, apart from injury, he has kept his place ever since. At the time of writing he was closing in upon a century of starts for Gloucester.

Rob loved the team camaraderie and the fervent supporters in Cornwall and, although Kingsholm with its famous Shed is an amazing place to play, he holds his time with the Pirates in huge affection.

He sees his longer term future in coaching both cricket and rugby and possibly in property development and to that end still retains a house in Penzance.

His fondest memories of his time at the Pirates included Worcester's Andy Goode getting yellow carded after Steve Winn had pulled his hair and hearing Alan Paver verbally winding up opposition front rows – especially when they came from Bristol.

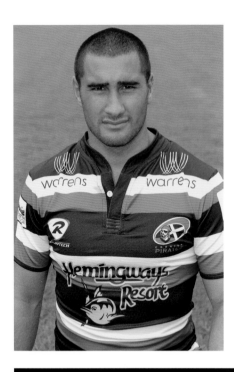

# Blair Cowan

Position: Back Row
Height/Weight: 6' 2", 16st 6lbs
Date of Birth: 1986
Matches: 54 + 23
Tries: 25

**Did you know?** Blair is an avid fan of Tolkien, the Lord of the Rings and The Hobbit and has a collection of all the books, DVDs and toys to prove it.

Scotland international Blair Cowan comes from a remarkable rugby family from Upper Hutt near Wellington in New Zealand. His Scottish credentials are nevertheless very strong as his mother was born and brought up in Blairmore in Argyllshire and only emigrated with her family when she was in her teens. His surname of Cowan can also be traced through his father's family back to Scotland.

His father had been a well-known lock forward who played for Upper Hutt as did Blair and his younger twin brothers who are both accomplished players. One has represented Canterbury and the Cook Islands (from where the family also trace their roots) and the other plays in Brisbane. Just to round it off his cousin Pekahou Cowan plays for Western Force in Perth and has gained several caps for the Wallabies.

Blair grew up alongside Jonny Bentley and, living only a couple of streets from each other, they both attended St Joseph's Primary School and then went on together to the local college St Patrick's where the rugby star was Tom Waldrom of Exeter Chiefs. Despite his rugby heritage Blair was just as keen on softball and naturally surfing to which he remains addicted. At St Patrick's he made his way up through the various age and weight divisions representing Wellington at Under 16, 19, 21 levels and it was there that he first came onto the radar of Chris Stirling who was then coaching the Wellington age group teams.

In 2003 he actually gave up rugby and went to Australia to do some surfing on the Gold Coast but then returned to train as a professional roofer. He still had no particular thought of playing rugby seriously but went along to his local club Upper Hutt chiefly to get himself fit. He soon made it into their first fifteen and the team (who included future All Black Cory

Jane) had their most successful season ever and won the coveted Swindale Shield for the first and only time. Two years later he was back at Wellington in their Academy and in the A team – once again working with Stirling.

When Stirling returned from a short visit to Cornwall to run his eye over the Pirates, Blair quizzed him about prospects in the UK. Stirling told him about the club and – just as importantly – how great the surf was in Cornwall. That all sounded pretty good to Blair. He had been recovering from injury and hadn't played for several months when he landed into a shivering wet British January. He was far from match fit but was immediately pitched into a cup match with Southend at Camborne. Fortunately Southend were a lower league team and sent packing without undue trouble although by the final whistle poor Blair was suffering badly from a combination of lack of training, the freezing cold and jet lag.

He had been brought in as a Number 8 and indeed this is where he played most of his rugby while with the Pirates. He had a good match at Rotherham but the club was going through one of its occasional troubled patches and, after an abject defeat in a cup tie at Nottingham a week later, the Head Coach Mark Hewitt lost his job. Only Stirling's long distance calming reassurances over the phone stopped Blair going straight back to roofing in New Zealand.

He saw out the season and a combination of Stirling's arrival with the Cornish summer sunshine and surf saw his life improve dramatically. He began the season with a fine performance against the Harlequins who boasted a back row of Robshaw, Easter and Skinner and then was a clear Man of the Match with a two try performance back at Nottingham. By this time he had been joined not only by his girlfriend from home but by his old mate Jonny Bentley and another Kiwi in Laurie McGlone.

That season saw him notch up fifteen tries from the middle of the back-row and be nominated into the Championship 'Dream Team'. He was also a key member of the team which won the inaugural B & I Cup at Camborne against Munster.

The Pirates enhanced their back-row options during the summer with the signing of Albion skipper Kyle Marriott and Phil Burgess. Blair began well enough but then picked up a nagging knee injury. Stirling had a policy of team rotation and used this to allow Blair to undergo a routine operation which unfortunately did not work and a second operation followed by a long lay-off kept him out from late January for the rest of the season. As a result he missed out on all the Championship play-offs and the exciting two-legged final with Worcester Warriors.

The following autumn he was able to play again but was still building up back to full fitness. He was in and out of the team but by Christmas he had got himself to a level where he was both playing well and ready to re-sign for the Pirates. Certainly he wanted to perform in the Premiership but with the team building up an impressive head of steam (they were to reach a second playoff final) and a stadium in Truro tantalisingly close he, along with the rest of the squad, wanted to play a continuing part of the Cornish Pirates story. Indeed he had recently turned down an approach from Sale Sharks.

Just at the moment that the golden opportunity for a stadium was to be shot down by the myopic politicians in Truro, Richard Hill of Worcester came in with an offer to play in the Premiership and join his pal Sam Betty at Sixways. Accordingly Blair decided to leave and had two seasons in the Premiership with over twenty Premiership starts and has particularly fond memories of beating the Saracens. However, he missed the sea and

Cornwall and in his second season was often side-lined by a pressurised Hill so it was with some relief that he moved to London Irish.

The Irish were coached by Kiwi Glenn Delaney who, as the head man at Nottingham, had long admired Blair and furthermore wanted him as a specialist flanker. It has proved to be a brilliant move for all concerned and he was soon getting regular Premiership rugby in a team which was not constantly battling against relegation as had been the case at Worcester. As a result he soon came to the notice of Scotland's Vern Cotter and he was given his first outing in the Scotland A team against the England Saxons in Glasgow. In the summer of 2014 he was capped for the first time against the United Sates in Houston and gained further caps against Canada and Argentina.

A big personal highlight was when his mother travelled back to her native Scotland to watch Blair take on Richie McCaw and the rest of the All Blacks at Murrayfield that autumn. The Cowan family had by then produced three international rugby players with different national teams but none of them had appeared for their home country of New Zealand. However, to a Kiwi boy from Upper Hutt this must have been a very special experience.

In the spring of 2015 he appeared in every minute all of Scotland's Six Nations matches and at the time of writing has played in eleven full internationals. The Scotland team suffered and lost all five matches but Blair regularly got high marks for his personal performances and – bar injury – should soon be playing a major part in the World Cup.

Life has turned out well for him with a new three-year contract at London Irish and plans to get married in the summer of 2016 in the beautiful Cook Islands. As with so many ex-Pirates, he gets down to Cornwall whenever he can to see his old mates and keep in touch. Some of the individual matches may begin to slip from the memory but the sense of camaraderie he felt in what he describes as a 'proper rugby club' will remain with him for years.

# Tim Cowley

Position: Back Row/ Lock
Height/Weight: 6'2", 16st 3lbs
Date of Birth: 1978
Matches: 66 + 19
Tries: 13

**Did you know?** Tim played for Samoa alongside his fellow Pirate Iva Motusaga.

Tim Cowley is a tough and popular New Zealander who hails from the town of Tokoroa in a forestry area of Waikato. Throughout his career at the Pirates he could always be relied upon to do a fine job anywhere at the back of the scrum. Despite being only just over 6 feet tall he won a lot of line-out ball as well as being a hard uncompromising tackler and a swashbuckling leader never happier than when he had a real battle on his hands.

Back in New Zealand he had played for a local club called Silverdale but followed his elder brother to represent the famous North Harbour team – a club sufficiently strong to have produced many All Blacks and considered highly enough to have had fixtures against the British Lions on their own account. He had started rugby aged only five and for the next ten years went up through the age and weight groups both with his club and Cambridge School in Waikato.

He also played sevens for the Waikato region when it won the national title for two successive years. He then went on a representative Under 21 Tour to Canada, the USA and Wales in a team that included the future legendary All Black prop Carl Hayman.

Furthermore through his father he qualified to play for Manu Samoa at both the fifteen and the seven-a-side versions of the game. In 2000 he obtained three caps for Samoa by playing against Japan, Canada and Italy.

As a youngster Tim was keen on all sports and took part in rugby league, boxing and squash. For a while he actually stopped playing rugby to concentrate on his boxing but was soon lured back to it. Having left school, he qualified as a carpenter and entered into the building trade. As with many young Kiwis, Tim wanted to see a bit of the world and although the season was already about to begin he landed a part-time contract with the Manchester club supplementing his salary working as a builder.

He made his debut well into the autumn but soon came to the Pirates' notice when he led an otherwise mediocre Manchester team against them at Grove Park. If the Manchester team were not very good the Pirates that day were frankly woeful and Cowley stood out like a beacon as he led his club to one of their precious few victories that season.

When they came to Cornwall for the return fixture already doomed to relegation, it was again Tim who seemed to be the one man taking on the Pirates eyeball to eyeball. The Pirates' management could hardly fail to be impressed and he proved to be one of Kevin Moseley's last but very best signings. At the time Tim was unsure about whether to return to New Zealand but the prospect of both playing for an ambitious club and living back near the sea proved hard to resist

He made his debut against the Cornish All Blacks in August 2004 and his first start in the Championship was at Nottingham the following month. A bad injury to Matt Evans early in that game gave him his first proper chance for a run in the team and he grabbed it with both hands in a battling win against Exeter.

During his first year he was in and out of the team and made as many appearances off the bench as it he did in the starting line-ups. The apparent turning point from being merely a useful squad member to an EDF Trophy winner and inspiring captain seemed to come about in the most unlikely circumstances. Matches between Otley and the Pirates had a history of flaring up and various referees had issued a number of red and yellow cards to both sides over the previous couple of years. Tim came off the bench but was soon red carded following two other yellows for Winn and Cracknell as a Pirates eight match winning streak came to a bad-tempered ending.

He served a short suspension but then came storming back at Birmingham & Solihull in vile weather to score two tries and stand out in a close victory. Within a month he captained the team in Cattle's absence against Moseley and by the time the EDF Trophy run began he was a permanent fixture. He took a knock in a televised match with Rotherham and missed the semi-final but was back and in his place for the match up with Exeter in the final at Twickenham.

Having starred in the back-row in that EDF final victory alongside the Canadian Stan McKeen and his great pal Iva Motusaga, he took over from Gavin Cattle as captain that summer when the Welshman went off to Llanelli Scarlets. He began with a friendly against Leicester and his first Championship match in charge was at Launceston when he got the crucial try in a surprisingly close battle. Tim seemed to revel in the big occasion and he never played better than in the three high pressure matches with Northampton Saints. When he finally left to try his luck with Bourgoin-Jallieu in France many Pirates fans were dismayed to see him go.

He harboured a dream to play Top Fourteen rugby and certainly realised that ambition with over forty appearances. Bourgoin-Jallieu had to struggle to retain their place at that level but Tim had the opportunity to play against the best and grabbed it with both hands. He would have had many more matches had it not been for the fact that his rugby in France was badly disrupted by injuries. The first and most serious was when he clashed heads with a teammate in a match at Toulouse and was knocked unconscious for several minutes. He was on the side-lines for months and then his comeback was interrupted by a serious neck injury which required an operation.

After leaving Bourgoin-Jallieu he had two more years with a club called Saint Médard en Jalles in the Gironde region and finally with a Level Three club named Mérignac which was where he decided finally to call it a day.

He had developed a particular love of Bordeaux – both the city and the wine – and, having retired from rugby, moved there and now runs a business providing local wine tours. Having become happy with the language and loving the lifestyle he appears to have settled in France and recently became the proud father of twins.

# Wes Davies

Position: Wing/Full Back
Height/Weight: 6' 2", 15st 4lbs
Date of Birth: 1978
Matches: 127 + 7
Tries: 48

**Did you know?** When the eleven-year-old Wes got his medal at Wembley it was presented to him by Coronation Street's Michael Le Vell.

Wesley Stephen Davies was born into the very heart of rugby league country in Wigan. His uncle had been a good player but his maternal grandfather was the immortal Billy Boston. Despite his celebrity, the great man was a quiet person who found that when he began to watch young Wes play he got so many fans wanting to talk to him that he found it almost impossible to follow the match.

Wes began playing when he was ten at St Jude's School and soon represented Wigan Under 11s. The little lads had the massive thrill of appearing at Wembley to play a curtain raiser before the Cup final and then meeting the Wigan stars afterwards. Moving on to St Thomas More Secondary school he continued to represent the town but a broken collar bone led to an extended layoff.

Nevertheless before long he was in the Wigan Youth and Academy teams playing mainly as a fly-half or centre. He got his first big chance in 1998 when he came off the bench at Salford and was handed a debut try by a perfect pass from Jason Robinson. To add to the occasion the match was televised and a big party ensued at Billy Boston's pub afterwards to watch the recording.

All in all Wes had about fifty first team outings over the next two years but suffered a bitter disappointment when he was omitted from a grand final staged at Old Trafford due to a supposed lack of match fitness after returning from injury. During this time he had gained several rugby league caps for Wales and took part in a League World Cup appearing against the Kiwis at the Millennium Stadium in Cardiff and having already travelled to Pretoria to face South Africa in a pre-tournament friendly.

After that World Cup, Wes was persuaded to transfer to rugby union with Orrell who at the time were the property of the sportswear tycoon David Whelan who also owned Wigan's football and rugby league teams simultaneously. He was now at full-back and did well in a sport that was all somewhat strange to a newcomer. He moved briefly back to rugby league with Salford Reds and played a few months for them but, after feeling let down over his contract, moved back to the union code with Worcester.

He had a full season at Sixways and actually scored a hat-trick of tries against the newly-promoted Pirates in a runaway victory. That summer Dicky Evans was working to strengthen the squad and looked towards Worcester to help him do so. Wes was consequently one of four men duly bound for Cornwall along with Rhodri McAtee, Matt Evans and Duncan Murray.

His signing actually took place in Kenya where he had been playing in the Tusker Sevens watched by Evans who must have liked what he saw and signed him up. Although Wes has now settled in Cornwall, he knew virtually nothing of the place before he arrived but soon found himself working with the creative Jim Mackay and for eighteen months was a regular either at full-back or in the centre where he became the top try-scorer.

During his second season he endured a torrid time at The Stoop when the Harlequins gave the Pirates' pack a working over and later in the season was injured in an unexpected defeat by the more modest Sedgeley Park and so finished the season on the side-lines.

While he was at Orrell he had been capped for the Wales A team coached by Clive Griffiths and it was he who was now managing Doncaster. It was that connection which took Wes back northwards but to the other side of the Pennines. Over the following three years he was again their leading try-scorer and played around eighty times for the Knights including several matches against the Pirates. These were always highly charged affairs for him – so much so that once at Camborne he uncharacteristically managed to pick up a red card for an altercation with his old teammate Rhodri McAtee.

In 2009 both he and Gavin Cattle returned to Cornwall like prodigal sons and he had four more happy seasons with the Pirates. His wife Alex is the daughter of Rod Coward who had been installed as the Pirates' CEO and so his return to Cornwall was both a family and a rugby reunion.

By this time Wes was one of the senior brigade and was nicknamed 'The Old Rolls Royce' by another teammate – Tom Luke – but his pace, sidestep, rugby sense and strength were as a evident as ever. He began in his old position at full-back but with the advent of Rob Cook began to appear more regularly on the wing which was a position he did not enjoy as much although it brought him plenty of tries.

With Cook injured, Wes was back in his favourite shirt for the B & I Final at Camborne and turned in a vintage display but it was back on the wing the following year including in the playoff final against Worcester. He was unlucky to miss out the following year against London Welsh with a nagging Achilles injury.

He had one last season when again he got plenty of time in the team but decided to finally call it a day going out with a win against Jersey at the Mennaye by which time he was approaching 150 matches for the Pirates.

Since retiring from rugby he and his young family still live near Helston where he is a carpenter with plans to run his own business.

# Alberto Di Bernardo

Position: Fly Half
Height/Weight: 6' 0", 13st 0lbs
Date of Birth: 1981
Matches: 31 + 2
Tries: 2

Did you know? As a youngster, Alberto played soccer for Newell's Old Boys – the club that produced Lionel Messi. Alberto is a few years older than Messi but he did play with Gabriel Heinze of Manchester United and Real Madrid.

Alberto was born in Rosario, which is the second city in Argentina, into a family of Italian descent. His father ran a pharmacy and had played rugby as a prop forward. He joined a local team with the slightly confusing name of the Jockey Club when he was a mere five years old but rugby was not his only sport. In fact he played football until he was twelve and was only induced to switch to rugby by his father.

Rugby is a very popular game in Argentina but of course football is even more so – indeed it is a national obsession. In his teens Alberto played both and signed for the junior team of another famous Argentinian club called Newell's Old Boys. He was nearly twenty by the time he decided to concentrate entirely upon rugby.

By then he had played for the Pumas at Under 18 and Under 19 levels and in 1999 travelled to Wales to compete in the Under 19 World Cup appearing against the Welsh, France and Italy. Over the next two years he represented his country at Under 21 level and twice toured to Australia and New Zealand. On his second appearance in New Zealand in the Argentina Number 10 shirt he found himself being marked by a fiery open-side flanker who turned out to be Richie McCaw. The Pumas youngsters were soundly defeated but the Junior All Blacks had also included future stars like Carl Hayman, Jerry Collins and Mils Muliaina so this was hardly to be unexpected.

Rugby was still very much an amateur sport in Argentina and many of their players were coming to Europe to earn a living from the game. With an Italian grandfather, Alberto could easily qualify to work in Italy and so it was through a friend of the family that he began with a small club called Leonessa. He soon transferred to the senior Italian club L'Aquila who are based in a city of that name close to Rome.

While there he was selected for Italy A and also got the chance of playing in a European tournament which included a match against Newcastle Falcons. This whetted his appetite for playing in the English Premiership and his agent began working on this task. However with only twelve clubs in the Premiership and because neither the Jockey Club nor L'Aquila could be classed as household names in England at the time he was not immediately successful. Alberto was a gifted runner and kicker of a rugby ball with a solid defence but was probably going to have to prove himself at a lower level first

Fortunately Jim McKay saw plenty to admire in Alberto's DVD and before long he had landed in London and was on the seemingly interminable train journey to Penzance. As with so many new Pirates recruits he was welcomed by Alan Paver and soon found himself ensconced in a friendly atmosphere with some talented rugby players around him.

In fact he was only to be in Cornwall for a single season but his impact was sensational. After a couple of cameo appearances outside Rhodri Wells in pre-season friendlies, he burst onto the scene in the Pirates' very first match at Camborne notching up fourteen points in comfortably beating Otley. However, a week later the team came back down to earth with a bump having given an insipid display to be deservedly beaten by a very modest Waterloo team at Blundellsands. Alberto himself looked tentative and can hardly have relished the experience.

By the next match all this was forgotten as he was the star turn in ripping Moseley to shreds with a personal tally of thirty-two points including two fine tries of his own. All through that winter he continued to be the catalyst for all the Pirates achieved. He had all the necessary attributes of a fly-half including an eye for a break plus a very solid kicking game both from hand and as a place kicker at the posts. He performed particularly well at Leeds when the relegated Yorkshiremen won by only a single point in injury time and then again at Doncaster a fortnight later when he showed all the assurance of a Ronan O'Gara as he repeatedly forced the Knights into scrambling backwards.

Where he particularly excelled was in his temperament and his seemingly unflappable demeanour even under intense pressure. This was never more apparent than in the EDF Trophy match held in arctic conditions at Headingley when he unblinkingly converted Paver's late try to snatch victory in the dying seconds of a nail-biting struggle.

Within weeks he had signed for a suitably impressed Leeds for the season to follow and for a while his place was taken by Jimmy Moore. He came back from the replacements' bench in the televised match against Rotherham and then did likewise in the Trophy semi-final against Plymouth Albion at Camborne. It had been another close struggle until Alberto settled matters with two enormous drop goals.

In the final at Twickenham it was once again his boot which brought home the spoils with four successful penalties contributing to a famous 19-16 victory over Exeter Chiefs. It was a boiling hot day and he again showed all his innate ability to control the game by the way he nursed his pack to steer them home. Although he has gone on to play international rugby and returned to Twickenham the following season with Leeds, Alberto still recalls this as one of the highlights of his career.

He had quickly formed a fine half-back partnership with Gavin Cattle and had amassed no less than 331 points in a mere thirty-three matches. It was soon apparent that he would probably be moving up to the Premiership and both Gloucester and Exeter had expressed interest before Leeds, no doubt mightily impressed by the damage he had done to them, secured his signature.

Once up at Headingley he was joined by Vili Ma'asi and the ex-Pirate Richard Welding. Despite the fact that the Yorkshiremen were immediately relegated, Alberto nevertheless scored 127 points in the League and a further sixty-seven in Europe. The following year both he and Welding returned to Camborne against the Pirates where Leeds just prevailed for a breathless 25-23 victory and then repeated the dose late in the season back in Yorkshire. He was also back at Twickenham for a second EDF win when Leeds overcame Moseley.

After two seasons he joined Tim Cowley at Bourgoin-Jallieu in France. The Top Fourteen is a league which all southern hemisphere players yearn to experience and Alberto enjoyed the modern stadiums, big passionate crowds and not least the kinder weather. One highlight was a victory over a star-studded Toulouse.

Two years later he was on the move again – this time back to Italy and Treviso in the Celtic League. His first season was badly affected by a nagging ankle injury but after a year he finally got the international recognition he must have craved. Italy selected him for their tour to South Africa where he gained three caps, not only against the Springboks at Loftus Versfield, but also versus Scotland and Samoa. The following year he got one more against the Wallabies in Turin facing a team whose backs were coached by his old Pirates boss Jim McKay.

He has now returned to his roots in Rosario and rejoined both his old Jockey Club friends and the family pharmacy business. He has done some kicking coaching and still has many warm memories of his time in Cornwall and also recalls having his old teammates Paver, Cattle and Cowley visiting him at his home in Argentina a few years ago.

# Colin Dymond

Position: Back Row
Height/Weight: 6' 0", 13st 10lbs
Date of Birth: 1949
Matches: 520
Tries: 56

**Did you know?** Colin's nickname of 'Dumbo' was given to him by a workmate at Holman's Dry Dock and began simply as 'Dymo'.

Colin Steven Tregonning Dymond was not a big man by the standards of modern back-row forwards – but for all that he was a typical Cornish creation with the heart of a lion and as hard as granite.

Colin's father worked in copper mining and was based at the mining town of Luanshya in Zimbabwe where Colin was born and indeed all his early childhood was spent in East Africa. There were no rugby players in the family although his grandfather had once been a steward at the Mennaye. They all returned to Cornwall to settle in Pendeen when Colin was about ten. His father worked briefly at Geevor mine and, although he then went for a while to Malaya, the rest of the family remained at Pendeen thereby allowing him to become properly Cornish.

His secondary school Cape Cornwall at St Just had only played football but their PE master was Derek Small – a tough Pirates forward of the 1940s and 50s very much in the mould of Colin himself. Small got rugby started and was an inspiration to his keen, fit young pupil who seemed to have found a sport which really suited him.

He thus arrived in the summer of 1965 at the pre-season training of Mounts Bay Colts and it was immediately obvious that his tackling and general work rate would, if channelled properly, produce something a bit special. The coach was Ken Thomas whose dedicated work saw dozens of young lads through the early stages of their Pirate careers. Thomas used him wisely, played him in a number of different positions and within two years Colin was making his first team debut.

This was on the wing alongside fellow Mounts Bay product Dudley Richards against Newton Abbot on The Mennaye in September 1967. The club had endured a difficult start to the season but that afternoon chalked up their first victory. The following week he was there again as another good win was recorded at Redruth but then a weakened Pirates team took a hammering at Plymouth Albion and it was back to the reserves for Colin to continue his rugby education.

His career took a distinct upturn the following season when he decided to concentrate on the back-row and for the rest of his career he played either as a flanker or as a Number 8. It was in this latter position that he began with a tough baptism against Cornwall's champion team of the time which was Penryn who supplied the core of the county team at that time. He did well and there was no disgrace in a narrow 6-8 defeat.

He got a more torrid introduction to the darker arts of the back-row a couple of weeks later when the Pirates faced a touring team known as The Tankards and Colin found himself up against the vastly-experienced British Lions and Ireland flanker Noel Murphy. However he learned from the experience and was soon forging a good understanding with open-side flanker John White. At the time the Pirates were not at their strongest so a huge amount of work fell upon the back-row defence but Colin invariably rose to the occasion.

Over the next few seasons he was an automatic selection whenever he was available. He also seemed to enjoy a relatively charmed life with regard to injuries – unlike the repeatedly luckless White.

As his progress continued one might have expected more interest from Cornwall's selection committee. Although they had two exceptional back-row candidates available in Peter Hendy and Roger Corin, the third place seemed to be permanently up for grabs and quite why Colin was only required to fill it on a mere two occasions will ever remain a mystery. He did get his chance when Devon came to Redruth in November 1972 and he performed creditably enough in a narrow 15-19 defeat. He got one further chance a month later in a friendly match against the Navy at Devonport but that appeared to be it. He was never to be called upon again.

As he matured, he took on more responsibility and frequently led the pack but it was in the Cornwall Cup that he probably reached the high point of his rugby career. The competition had been reintroduced in the late 1960s with very little fanfare but, apart from a single semi-final appearance at Penryn in 1970, the Pirates had never covered themselves in glory.

In March 1975 they reached a final with Penryn at Camborne. Preparation had been chaotic with the bus being held up and, through arriving late and the need for a lot of pre-match photos and presentations, the team was 'flat' when they emerged to play. So, despite the best efforts of the back-row of Colin, White and Phil Westren they fell short at the last hurdle.

A year later it was a totally different story. Club captain David Drew had been injured and Colin as his vice-captain thus took over. Having already disposed of Falmouth and Penryn, he led the team through a dramatic replayed semi-final with Hayle to meet a powerful Redruth in the Final itself.

Colin reflected on the tension in the dressing room before the match. On paper the Reds were unquestionably the stronger outfit but there was a grim determination among the Pirates that history with all those pre-match distractions should not be repeated.

Camborne Recreation Ground was alive with nearly 5,000 thronging the old ground. The teams battled themselves to a standstill and the match was only won in high drama when big lock Alan Reynolds thundered up field to offload via Neil Care to that flying winger Nobby Roberts who tore away to register the only try of the match. Stack Stevens had only recently finished his England career the previous season but this was one of his greatest ever games for the club and he inspired those around him to play far beyond themselves.

Colin had led the Pirates to possibly their finest moment for at least fifteen years and the celebrations continued long into the night. The champagne had been left unopened from the previous season but it was now put to full use.

On the strength of this victory the Pirates qualified for their first-ever foray into a national knock-out competition taking on the Gloucester club Gordon League at The Mennaye in the John Player Cup. Hopes ran high but sadly it was not to be and Colin had to endure the frustration of his team missing out by a single point and thus being eliminated in the very first round.

It was therefore only natural that he would captain the club in his own right the following season although, apart from some creditable victories over Taunton and Redruth coupled with an interesting fixture with the American touring team Kansas City Jayhawks, it was not an outstanding one.

With a young family he needed to find more lucrative employment than working in Holman's Dry Dock and so he took a job as a derrick man on the North Sea oil rigs flying regularly between Cornwall and the Shetland Isles to do so. The rigs banned alcohol but always had a gymnasium available and he therefore found little difficulty keeping himself fit. He continued to play for the Pirates whenever he was back at home and found he was able to slip back into the groove without undue difficulty.

In January 1982 he suffered a minor setback when he was sent off at Taunton for stepping in and retaliating when his jumper, the feisty ex-Cardiff forward Roger Lane, had been repeatedly fouled in the line-outs. As his colleague Lane was clearly big and tough enough to look after himself, Colin always felt this a little ironic.

He continued playing well into the 1980s and – by the time he eventually called it a day in 1985 – he had joined that very select group of players who have represented Penzance and Newlyn more than 500 times.

He gave up the oil rigs in 1990 and returned to Penzance where he was able to watch his son play for the Pirates Colts and South West schools as a promising fly-half.

In recent years he has worked as a groundsman both at the Mennaye and at Camborne. He is still seen regularly around the club on match days where his forthright views on all things rugby and those who play or administer it are always well worth listening to.

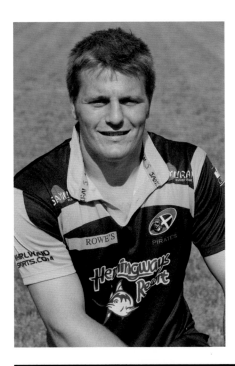

# Rob Elloway

Position: Hooker
Height/Weight: 6'0", 16st 0lbs
Date of Birth: 1983
Matches: 123 + 64
Tries: 16

Did you know? Despite Rob's assertion that he has only ever played six games of rugby other than at hooker, he made his international debut for Germany as a replacement flanker.

Robert Kevin Elloway's family are from Heywood on the outskirts of Rochdale but, with a father serving in the forces, he was born on an army base at Rinteln close to Hameln in Germany. His early childhood involved shuttling between Lancashire and Germany but he eventually settled back in Heywood where he started his rugby career playing mini rugby league.

Already established as a hooker, he switched over to union when he and a friend joined Sedgeley Park RFC near Radcliffe – a club familiar to travelling Pirates fans. He was spotted by ex-England full-back Simon Hodgkinson and accordingly was offered a scholarship to the prestigious Sedbergh College a well-known rugby playing public school which has produced at least three famous England rugby captains in John Spencer, Will Carling and Lord Wakefield.

From this rugby hothouse he played for Lancashire schools at every level and then was selected by the northern-based coach Geoff Wappett for the England Under 18 team gaining caps against Wales, Ireland, Scotland and France.

On the strength of this he was recruited by Nigel Melville to join the Gloucester Academy as a young professional. It was at this stage that he acquired his nickname 'Pot' bequeathed to him by Chris Fortey, a grizzled old Kingsholm front-rower, who declared Rob's new haircut looked like he had a pot on his head.

As a teenage hooker having to compete with experienced internationals like Oliver Azam and Mefin Davies, he obviously found Premiership chances limited. Nevertheless a series of injuries gave him an early opportunity to come off the bench at Kingsholm against London Irish and to take on Naka Drotsky the ex-Springbok hooker. Furthermore being in the constant company of experienced front-row men taught him a great deal and he honed his reliable throwing-in skills with help from Mefin Davies.

He remained at Kingsholm for five seasons and made about twenty-five first team appearances with seven starts including matches against Munster and Saracens. As with every Gloucester player, he found playing in front of the Shed a thrilling experience but also got to play in Toulon and Bucharest

As he finished his fifth year his coach Dean Ryan was ready to release him. Ryan admired Rob's abilities and so recommended him to Mark Hewitt who had been his Academy coach at Gloucester but was by now the forwards' coach at the Pirates. Rob knew nothing about Cornwall but, liking what he found, signed on as the replacement for Vili Ma'asi who had just departed for Leeds Carnegie.

Following in the footsteps of Ma'asi, the try hero of Twickenham, was always going to be a challenge. His debut was in a pre-season friendly with Leicester Tigers but then his Championship career got off to a flying start when the tough and mobile 'Potty' announced his presence with a superb try in front of a packed house at Camborne against Northampton Saints.

That was a dramatic introduction when, inspired by a rampaging Tim Cowley, the Pirates ripped into the illustrious Saints and Rob renewed an acquaintance with another young man in the opposing front-row named Dave Ward. The two had actually met and battled it out before in matches between Gloucester's A team and that of Bath where the ebullient Ward had then been based. They again enjoyed a rare old duel and each had scored a try for their respective teams by the finish.

The Pirates had also signed an older, and possibly more experienced, hooker in the Kiwi Nathan Kemp from Jersey but Rob soon became the first choice. However once Ward had signed two years later he found there was now going to be massive competition for the starting hooker's shirt.

By this time Rob had decided to use his German birthplace and qualification to play some international rugby for Germany and picked up a couple of caps in the process. These came against Russia in Hanover and Rumania by the Black Sea in Constanta. The German team were probably not playing at anywhere near the standard of the Pirates but the experience was still a rewarding one. On the debit side it now ruled him out from being considered as an English Qualified Player (EQP) under the newly-introduced rules of the Rugby Union despite having played for England as a schoolboy.

With regard to the Elloway-Ward rivalry, there was a clear contrast in styles between them. Each in their own way was as effective as any in the Championship at the time and certainly the best pair to pick from by a country mile. While Ward had supporters and referees shaking their heads in wonder at his ball-stealing tactics and weaving runs, Rob appeared a little bigger and stronger, threw the ball in more consistently and probably conceded fewer penalties. Unlike Rob, who had never played anywhere other than as a hooker, Ward could operate equally effectively in the back-row. In the triumphant B & I Cup final against Munster at Camborne, Stirling solved the issue by playing them both with brilliant results.

Over the next three seasons he had to compete with the continuing pyrotechnics of Ward but always more than held his own. In the two-legged final of the Championship playoffs against Worcester it was Ward who had the starting role in the first leg in Penzance but the situation was reversed a week later before a 12,000 crowd at Sixways.

Once Ward left for the Harlequins, Rob's position seemed settled but in both of the succeeding seasons he picked up neck injuries which limited his matches. For a time Jack Yeandle of Exeter Chiefs covered for him and then another back-row-cum-hooker was signed in the person of the Canadian skipper Aaron Carpenter followed by Tom Channon from Bath.

Despite all this Rob, who is now in his early thirties which is when hookers are still in their prime, has just passed the 200 matches mark in Pirate colours. He was selected for the Barbarians against Clontarf just outside Dublin and had two loan spells – one at Bournemouth to help regain match fitness after an injury layoff and a second to aid London Welsh who were struggling at the foot of the Premiership.

He clearly loves Cornwall with a partner from Falmouth and has developing ambitions as a coach, having already worked and gained valuable experience with Hayle, St Ives and Redruth.

# Jimmy Glover

Position: Centre/Wing
Height/Weight: 6' 0", 13st 7lbs
Date of Birth: 1936
Matches: 144
Tries: 39

**Did you know?** Jimmy was elected Oxford captain in front of two future England captains in Richard Sharp and John Willcox plus F. E. R. Butler who later, as Sir Robin Butler, was to head the entire British Civil Service at the time of Margaret Thatcher.

Jimmy Glover was one of those all-round sportsmen we all rather envy who seemed to excel in everything he touched while at Penzance Grammar School in the 1950s. Rugby, tennis, football, athletics, golf and cricket all came easily to him. At tennis he often represented Cornwall with Peter Michell as his doubles partner.

He was born in Newlyn and his father had once captained the Penzance football team and so grew up in a sports-minded environment. In fact he played very little rugby as a youngster at school. Both Tolcarne Primary and the Grammar School concentrated on soccer and, unlike so many of his contemporaries, he was not a member of the Colts and Mounts Bay nurseries.

Hence when he did make his first team debut as a teenage centre against Falmouth in January 1955 he had actually played very little rugby. Once, when playing in a Cornwall Schools trial, a teammate had to tell him where to stand.

On leaving school he joined the RAF to do his National Service as a Pilot Officer and spent much of it in Cyprus during the EOKA terrorist period and also had to prepare transit facilities for troops departing for the Suez crisis.

His appearances for the Pirates meanwhile were extremely few and far between. However he had become available again in the summer of 1957 and returned at Jedburgh when the Pirates toured the Scottish Borders and that early autumn put in a number of scintillating performances.

Soon he was off again to Corpus Christi College at Oxford to study French and gained a place in the Greyhounds (essentially the University Second Fifteen) who often visited Penzance prior to Christmas when both he and Richard Sharp featured against the Pirates.

The following season he made his debut for Cornwall on the wing against Dai Gent's team at Falmouth and marked it with a well-taken try. He then got another chance when was selected against Gloucestershire at Bristol – a place he was going to get to know very well over the next few years.

However it was the season 1959/60 when his career really took off. By then he was bigger and stronger with excellent balance, solid handling skills and above all an astute rugby brain coupled with a rock solid defence. He finally broke through into the Oxford University team to win a coveted 'Blue' playing alongside England centre Malcolm Phillips (who advised him to be a winger) and the sometimes brilliant Sharp. Oxford won a rather dull match on penalties but Jimmy's star was clearly in the ascendancy. A few days later he scored a crucial try in a South West Division playoff at a packed Redruth outwitting Devon's star Mike Blackmore and helping Cornwall to win the group.

He was soon back at Twickenham with Cornwall for the semi-final against Surrey where he now found himself marking England's sprint champion and British Lion John Young. While Cornwall lost narrowly and somewhat unluckily, Jimmy again performed with credit.

University rugby played a much bigger part on the national stage in those amateur days when winning a Blue guaranteed close interest from the England selectors. It was therefore a feather in his cap to be elected to captain Oxford for the following season.

Before the Varsity match itself Jimmy led Oxford against the Springboks but, missing the injured Sharp, they were well beaten. This experience repeated itself at Twickenham where Cambridge came through with a bit to spare leaving a somewhat frustrated Jimmy to concentrate on getting his degree and thinking about his first teaching job. He still managed to return to Penzance for several matches including memorable ones with Wasps and Cardiff and scored a remarkable individual try to beat a strong Pontypool side on the Mennaye.

His first teaching job was at Clifton College which he had obtained largely on the promptings of the ex-Pirates star John Kendall-Carpenter. The great man had actually moved on just before Jimmy started thus giving him the opportunity of not only teaching rugby but also playing for Bristol. He was joined there by fellow Pirate and lock-forward David Mann and both were in a strong Cornwall team which swept through to the County Championship semi-finals where they lost out to an even more powerful Warwickshire who were going through a remarkable spell of successive wins. It was a mark of just how talented the Pirates were at that stage in that they comprised almost half of that particular Cornwall team.

Throughout the mid-1960s Jimmy played regularly against all the top sides for Bristol chalking up some 200 appearances for the club while at the same time he was more or less a fixture in the Cornwall team finally amassing forty-one appearances including three more semi-finals against Surrey in 1967.

On joining Bristol he had insisted upon switching from the wing to play most of his rugby as a constructive centre often alongside his former Oxford colleague Laurie Watts. His appearances in a Pirates shirt were rather spasmodic at this stage but he nevertheless came back home to Cornwall regularly in the school holidays and therefore could usually be seen around September, Christmas and Easter against the touring teams.

It was as a centre that he played for the South West Counties against Whineray's All Blacks at Exeter partnering England's Martin Underwood but for some reason higher representative honours always seemed to pass him by. He never appeared in an England Trial despite many lesser players doing so repeatedly.

His last season for Cornwall was in 1967/68 when he belatedly was asked to captain the side. This again seemed surprising as he had all the pedigree and rugby intelligence necessary to direct and channel Cornwall's traditionally rumbustious approach but the county selectors seemed to favour others such as Ron Glazsher to whip their men into the fiery frenzy that all their thousands of supporters demanded. Often it worked but there were key moments in close but losing matches when the cool leadership of a Jimmy Glover might just have carried them through.

In April 1968 Jimmy was finally recognised with a call to join the Barbarians tour of South Wales appearing in the two plum fixtures against Cardiff and Swansea. He played alongside the current French star Jean Gachassin and the immortal Gareth Edwards.

As players approach the age of thirty and their best days are perhaps behind them many decide to pack it in. Jimmy however was of a different mind-set. He had always maintained a high standard of fitness even in the close season when his other sporting interests always kept him busy. He also seemed to be quite lucky with regard to injuries.

On leaving Clifton he taught at a comprehensive in Bristol and then moved to Swindon where he was persuaded to kick-start a revived rugby career with Swindon RFC and renewed his county rugby by turning out for Dorset & Wilts. Following an enjoyable spell teaching and playing in Malta, 1977 saw him give up teaching and return to Penzance. Initially he managed the Union Hotel and then moved back home to Newlyn to take over the Jelbert family ice cream business, get married and resettle in Cornwall.

In doing so he returned to play for the club for which he had made his debut some twenty-two years previously. He still loved playing and seemed to derive as much pleasure turning out for the second and third teams against the likes of St Day and St Just as he had in his glory days at Twickenham.

Jimmy's sporting genes have obviously been passed on to his famous daughter, Helen, who won Britain's first Gold Medal in the 2012 Olympics for rowing and has since added several other titles including European and World Championships.

Now as a remarkably fit-looking 'seventy something' – albeit with two new knees – he still enjoys his tennis and golf and follows rugby but feels it has somehow lost a bit of its old romance along the way.

# Martin Haag

Position: Lock
Height / Weight: 6' 6", 18st 0lbs
Date of birth: 1968
Matches: 43 + 7
Tries scored: 5

**Did you know? One of Martin's first jobs was packing sand eels at St Ives.**

Martin Haag was born in Chelmsford, Essex. His father worked for British Railways hotels and the family moved to St Ives when he was transferred to the Tregenna Castle Hotel.

St Ives has always been a rugby-loving town and, growing up there and attending the local comprehensive, he was naturally drawn to the minis and colts teams at the club. He was already a big lad with an obvious talent for the game and he was soon playing for Cornwall at Under 16 level.

When he went on to do his A Levels at Penwith College he developed rapidly and was selected to play for England at Under 18. It was suggested during the trials that, as there were a large number of back-row men available but a shortage of locks, Martin should switch to the middle row of the scrum. He agreed and was rewarded with caps against Wales, Ireland, France, Scotland and Australia in a side containing Neil Back and Tony Underwood.

By this time he was appearing for St Ives itself and the following season had his first taste of senior rugby when he was selected for Cornwall's semi-final against Middlesex at The Stoop. It was a big step up but he did well and it was obvious that the big clubs would take an interest Martin actually played one match for the Harlequins against Swansea and scored a try but when Jack Rowell and Graham Dawe asked him to come to Bath he soon decided that was indeed the place to be.

At the time Bath were clearly the best club team in England and arguably in the whole of Europe with a plethora of international players. In his first season he got sixteen starts but had to compete as a lock with Nigel Redman and Damian Cronin for his place. Rather as Exeter does today, Bath had many of the best Cornish players in their squad including not only Dawe but also Adrian Bick, Barry Trevaskis, Roger Spurrell and Ian Sanders soon to be joined by Andy Reed.

Rugby was of course still an amateur sport and Martin worked for Lloyd's Bank. He played for the South West in the ill-starred regional championships which served as virtual England trials, played for the England Under 23 team and continued to represent Cornwall. In 1989 he was in the back-row when Cornwall made the first of its Twickenham appearances where they lost narrowly to Durham. This was a big disappointment but thousands of black-and-gold clad rugby fans developed a taste for the Twickenham experience and this sowed the seeds for the great 'Cornish invasions' of 1991 and 1992.

Martin however was destined not to be there. Competition for places at Bath was ruthless and if a player was away for a week performing elsewhere he might have to wait months to get his place back and so had to decide where his priorities lay. Bath were on the crest of a wave and his final decision of placing club before county was almost inevitable.

His career at Bath lasted a remarkable fourteen seasons during which time he made 315 appearances for them and featured in three Pilkington Cup Finals scoring two tries in one against Wasps. He appeared for England at B level and for other representative teams all over the world including in Australia, New Zealand, Canada, South Africa, Zimbabwe, Dubai, Barbados and even Thailand.

For all that a full England cap still eluded him but in 1997 his chance finally arrived. The Lions were in South Africa but Rowell still took an England team devoid of the Johnsons, Guscotts and Dallaglios to Argentina. Martin was struggling with a neck injury at the time but went out anyway and belatedly became a full England player with two matches against the Pumas in Buenos Aires.

His playing days at Bath finished in 2001 and he began working with the Bath Academy and the Juniors which included a chirpy young man called Dave Ward. He still wanted to play and, following a meeting with Dicky Evans, it was agreed that he would continue to coach the youngsters at Bath but play and train as a part-timer for the Pirates.

He arrived with two other Bath lads, Ollie Hodge and Dan Seal, and his influence was immediately apparent. The Pirates had some brilliant attacking players but were not sufficiently well organised, especially in defence, and had twice missed out on promotion from National III when they should probably never have done so.

He made his debut at home against Blackheath alongside Richard Carroll and only missed three matches during the entire season claiming five tries in the process. He shared the captaincy duties with scrum-half Mark Roderick and was a key leader even when the Welshman was skippering the side. When promotion was at last secured against Westcombe Park in the leafy suburbs of Orpington it was Martin who was very much at the helm steering the boat home.

He missed the first few matches of season 2002/03 but came back into the side in late September. In the late autumn the Pirates went down sloppily to Henley Hawks but from then onwards won their last sixteen matches on the bounce to run away with the National Two title at the first time of asking.

Martin only had two seasons in Penzance but the club had gained successive promotions and his experience and steady hand had done much to channel the physical power and raw aggression of younger men like Carroll, Hodge, Kevin Penrose, Vili Ma'asi and Joe Bearman into a highly competitive forward unit.

Having gained promotion, the Pirates' management unaccountably did not renew his contract. Whatever their reasoning, the club came within an ace of bitterly regretting their decision. Faced with a whole new set of challenges in what was then known as National I and now being opposed by full-time professionals, it was found that the men initially recruited to replace him in the second-row were simply not up to the task. It was only with the arrival of Martin Morgan, Will James and Heino Senekal the following year that the balance was redressed.

Martin had by then returned to coaching, initially joining ex-Bath colleague Richard Hill at Bristol, taking the England Under 18s to Australia and managing the England Under 20s at the 2008 Junior World Cup in Japan. He then had another three-year stint at Bath before taking up his current position of Director of Rugby at Nottingham where he regularly comes face-to-face with the Pirates.

His family still lives in Bath where his son has already begun to play mini rugby. His parents remain in Cornwall and he gets down to visit them whenever he can. In some ways his highly successful and varied career both as a player and as a coach reflects the relative lack of facilities and opportunities for young men of his calibre existing back in Cornwall as not once but twice it appears he was the 'one who got away'.

Of course there have been far too many others before and since – but perhaps one day he will return.

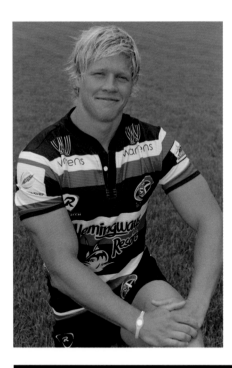

# Matt Hopper

Position: Centre
Height/Weight: 5'10", 14st 2lbs
Date of Birth: 1985
Matches: 33 + 3
Tries: 10

**Did you know?** Matt has a degree in criminology and considered a career in the police force.

Matthew Aaron Hopper only stayed for one season with the Pirates but his impact was instantaneous and he starred in what was arguably the best-ever Cornish Pirates team to date. Furthermore his subsequent career has been a spectacular success at the highest level.

He is the son of the old Exeter and Devon scrum-half Keith Hopper but it was actually his mother who took him along to play mini rugby with the Chiefs Under 10s. At Exeter School he progressed through the various age groups and led them in winning the Devon Schools Cup against Torquay in 2002 while also representing Devon, the South West and getting trials for England Schoolboys.

At this time he was playing most of his rugby as a full-back and occasional fly-half and his conversion to centre was only to come later. Although both Bath Academy and Harlequins Academy had already shown an interest in him, Matt decided to stay on at school and study for university.

On leaving school he did the popular thing and travelled to Australia, New Zealand and Fiji and, having returned home to Exeter, then played for Wessex RFC – a junior club in Exwick based at the engagingly named Flowerpot Field. Ironically, given his father's Exeter heritage and Matt's obvious prowess, the Chiefs have played little or no part in his career beyond his childhood.

At Cardiff University he studied Education and Criminology and at the same time his rugby career began to take off again. He was soon in the university team and was offered a contract with Pontypridd but changed his mind and signed for Newport. The rugby was exciting and the Welsh Varsity match pitching Swansea against Cardiff is keenly anticipated every year. He then featured for the Welsh Academicals and had trials for the English Universities team. He also grabbed the opportunity to play with his university in the Hong Kong 'Super Tens' competition. Ten-a-side rugby has never really taken off in the UK but Matt really loved it.

While at Cardiff he met his future wife and they were already engaged when they both took off back to Australia and stayed in Sydney. Matt hooked up with the famous Manly Club, initially in the Third Grade, but very soon was enjoying first team rugby and rubbing shoulders with Wallabies like George Smith and Phil Waugh. The Manly skills coach and ex-Rugby League man Phil Blake worked on his centre play and Matt was by then developing fast.

He might well have stayed longer but unfortunately suffered a bad bout of meningitis and so returned to England as soon as he was well enough to fly home. The 2008/09 season was already well under way by the time he was fit again and he was looking for a club. He knew Cornwall well from numerous family holidays as a child and conversations were held with Mark Hewitt but the Pirates already had a full squad and then, at the critical moment, Hewitt lost his job.

However, Graham Dawe signed him for Plymouth Albion basically as an amateur with a match fee payable whenever he actually played. After a couple of run-outs with the Second Team he appeared in a 'friendly' against the Combined Services and then made his Championship debut against Esher at Brickfields bagging two tries in the process. He stayed in the team from then onwards.

A great performance against the Pirates in the Championship play-offs the following season was shown live on Sky TV and suddenly everyone sat up and took notice of the exciting, aggressive centre with the blond locks and a bewildering sidestep. Neither Albion nor the Pirates progressed to the semi-finals but Chris Stirling lost no time in bringing Matt to accompany Kyle Marriott in signing for the Pirates.

He celebrated his debut against Gwent Dragons with a try in the closing minutes. The game was memorable in that the Pirates had just relocated at short notice back to Penzance and there had been a frantic scramble to get the ground ready just in time. Matt along with fellow debutants Marriott, Phil Burgess and Ian Nimmo all showed up well.

In fact he was one of the standout backs throughout the season and hardly missed a match. He was fortunate in that Jonny Bentley inside him was at the height of his powers and could prise open defences for Matt's aggressive running to be exploited to the full. This was never more apparent than in the Pirates' epic victory at Worcester when, sparked by the jinking Kiwi, Matt repeatedly ripped the Championship favourites apart in front of their own rather disgruntled supporters. He scored one breath-taking try and had another even better one ruled out on a marginal forward pass decision.

In defence he was tasked with getting up in the opposition's faces usually working with the ever-reliable Steve Winn to act as a form of 'sweeper' behind him. It generally worked well and Matt clearly profited from the steadiness and rocklike tackling of his elder partner. He also had the benefit of working closely with Harvey Biljon who spent hours hammering home the basics required to go alongside Matt's box-of-fireworks approach.

All in all he claimed ten tries including two doubles which was a fair total but his flamboyant attack also led to defences being diverted towards him and thus he gained space for others around him. His other attribute was that he obviously enjoyed getting stuck into the rucks and breakdowns and constantly looked for work. This has stood him in particularly good stead in his later Harlequins career.

Although a Devonian, Matt loves Cornwall with an engaging passion but the call of Premiership rugby in general, and the Harlequins in particular, was probably irresistible. Nevertheless he thought about it long and hard. His wife had begun a business running Pilates classes and the lure of Cornwall was strong but they made the break and, although a relatively late developer at top level, his career took off.

After an initial period recovering from injury and playing in the A team, he scored a neatly-taken try in his first big match against Gloucester. A fine performance in the Heineken Cup in Toulouse made people sit up and take serious notice while the blond Viking look proved popular with newspaper editors and his photograph was featured prominently in the press.

After a very short time he was selected for the England Saxons team but the England coaches seemed to favour the big men in the centre like Twelvetrees and Tuilagi when it came to selecting the senior squad. Fortunately Conor O'Shea at the Harlequins saw things rather differently and, despite the presence of men of the calibre of Lowe and Turner-Hall, Matt has appeared regularly over the past three years all over the UK and France.

In recent times he has become more calculating in his play with a heavy accent upon work rate, passing and solid defence in a well-rehearsed pattern. With the benefit of operating outside the outstanding Kiwi fly-half Nick Evans he has matured into an integral cog in a well-oiled Quins machine.

Having just passed his thirtieth birthday, but with an extended contract, he hopes to continue playing top level rugby for quite a while yet. He has trained to be a carpenter and would always be open to the prospect of coming back to Cornwall and the Pirates if all the circumstances were right.

# Will James

Position: Lock
Height/Weight: 6'6", 19st 0lbs
Date of Birth: 1976
Matches: 41+10
Tries: 2

Did you know? At school in Plymouth Will was a classmate of future Pirate Duncan Roke.

Big Will James is very much a man of Plymouth. His father had played local amateur football but both he and his brother came up through the ranks with Plymouth Albion where he started in the minis, worked his way up through the Under 13s and, as a boy at Plymouth College, made the England Schools A team at Under 16 age group in 1993 getting his cap against Spain.

He also figured in the England Schools squad at Under 19 level along with future Pirates Joe Beardshaw and Tom Barlow and was again capped against Italy. In 1995 he was recruited by Bath for their Youth Team under the direction of former Pirate hooker John Kimberley. He had by then left school and was working in a company which made tractor tyres but, as and when the sport went professional in 1996, he signed up on an Academy contract.

After eighteen months he was loaned out to Pontypool and before long formally signed for them. 'Pooler' were then in the second tier of clubs in Wales but had a magnificent history and Will had the honour of being elected as the youngest-ever captain of that proud club. Even then he was a big strong lad and the rough and tumble of Welsh club rugby served to toughen him up to the extent that a year later he was able to step up to the top tier in South Wales with Pontypridd. By this time he had decided that if any national honours were to come his way he would follow the Welsh side of his family and turn out for Wales. His two years at Pontypridd were very successful and he played in almost every match making over sixty appearances in doing so. He also got some European experience by turning out at places such as Toulouse, Dax, Agen and Colombiers.

His wife was also from Plymouth and they now had a young daughter. It was therefore no surprise that when Graham Dawe asked him to come back to his home city that he jumped at the chance. Albion was then a team built around a big powerful pack which included not only Dawe himself but Dan Ward-Smith, Wayne Reed and a youthful Alan Paver.

There is no doubt that they were successful and beat the Pirates several times during his three-year stint but a combination of a disappointing contract offer and an admiration for the way the Pirates were trying to play rugby persuaded him to sign up with Kevin Moseley and renew his acquaintance with Paver.

After a nerve-wracking first season in what was then known as National I, the Pirates knew they had to beef up their pack. With his huge frame and rippling muscles topped off by a gleaming bald head, Will immediately became the central hard core of what rapidly developed into an impressive set of forwards. Initially paired with Martin Morgan, he was soon joined by the big Namibian Heino Senekal and the Pirates could now front up to any pack in the Championship. In this regard two epic battles with the Baxter brothers at Exeter followed by another with Ed Pearce and Olly Hodge at Bristol told Pirates fans all they needed to know. Will and Heino were the real deal.

Will loved the Pirates' team spirit, the rugby and the supporters but did not enjoy the daily commute to training from his home in Plymouth involving a near 200 mile round trip. He was twenty-nine and still ambitious for Premiership rugby and so when Dean Ryan at Gloucester came looking Will could hardly fail to be interested. The Pirates were playing at Kenwyn that season and had made a fine start but by then were being outpaced by the Harlequins. Will had also been struggling with a groin injury which required surgery and by February he had turned out in a Pirate shirt for the last time.

He did not get into the Gloucester side immediately but came off the bench against Leinster in the January and then kept his place for the rest of the season. A LV Cup win, a Premiership final and dozens of other big matches in the UK and Europe followed in their turn and he formed impressive partnerships with Alex Brown, Marco Bortolami and latterly England lock Dave Attwood. Several Pirates followed his path to Kingsholm – most notably Darren Dawidiuk and Rob Cook.

In 2007 he was on holiday in France when he had the great thrill of being contacted to join the Wales squad preparing for the World Cup that autumn. His debut that summer at Twickenham was not a happy occasion for Wales who were thumped by a rampant England and conceded over sixty points. Fortunately he survived this traumatic experience and was retained for the tournament itself. He appeared at the Millennium Stadium off the bench against Argentina and France and finally had a starting place against Japan thus ending with four caps to his credit.

In the spring of 2014 he decided to retire although he could possibly have had one more season had he wished to do so. By this time he was thirty-seven years old and had made almost 200 first team appearances. He had been Gloucester's representative on the Rugby Players Association and had been its chairman and was thus well aware of the need to anchor down a longer term career. Consequently he bowed out at Kingsholm when playing against London Irish in the early May.

On retiring from Gloucester he took up an appointment as Head of Rugby and Sports Performance at Ampleforth College which is a famous Catholic Independent school in a beautiful part of North Yorkshire where he directs all rugby matters. One of the players the school produced a few years ago was Lawrence Dallalglio but who would bet against Will finding and developing another?

Away from rugby Will is very much a family man with teenage daughters and his outside hobby is playing the drums.

# Jimmy Jenkin

Position: Utility Forward
Height/Weight: 6'0", 14st 8lbs
Date of Birth: 1930
Died: 2002
Matches: 329
Tries: 27

**Did you know?** While serving with the RAF in Germany Jimmy took part in the historic Berlin airlift.

Jimmy Jenkin was born and grew up in Mousehole where his father was a fisherman and he was the eldest of three brothers. He went to Penzance Grammar School during the war at a time when no rugby was played but nevertheless was clearly a strong young athlete who could play football and excelled at running the half-mile. He did so well at that particular event that he ran in the National Schools Championships at the White City in London.

He had a brief spell with the young Mounts Bay team but soon made his debut for the seniors against the Old Paulines as a flanker in April 1947. He had a few more games that season and, by the time the following one came around, he was more or less a regular member of the back-row where he often appeared alongside the redoubtable John Kendall-Carpenter and Henry Care.

He was then called up for National Service and entered the RAF. As a result he was away from the Pirates until Christmas 1949 when he returned against Camborne. His real comeback was at Easter when he earned a place in club history by scoring the only try of the match against Cardiff to defeat their famous visitors by 5-0. It was a great occasion as Cardiff attacked relentlessly while the huge crowd cheered themselves hoarse.

Afterwards Cardiff's captain Frank Trott sportingly presented the Pirates' skipper Tinker Taylor with a Cardiff shirt which adorned the clubhouse for years. The real hero of the hour however was Jimmy.

It was now time for him to become qualified for his chosen profession of school teaching and he followed the well-trodden path to Exeter and St Luke's College. In September he made his debut for Cornwall against the British Police at the Mennaye, again in the back-row, when he showed up well against the then current Wales flanker Alan Forward.

He was now only available during college holidays and, by the time he returned at Christmas, he found himself in the second-row and this continued at Easter when he renewed acquaintance with the men from Cardiff. The previous year many of their stars had been on a ship to New Zealand with the British Lions but this time they brought their full array and over 8,000 crammed into the Mennaye to greet them. The game ended in a breathless 3-3 draw which in some ways was an even greater achievement than the victory of the previous year.

Jimmy was one of those invaluable team members who will do whatever job is required and could turn in a fine performance anywhere in the pack. That year the Pirates were invited to the Middlesex Sevens and Jimmy and Kendall-Carpenter propped Jack Gunn to form the Pirates forward trio. It was a proud moment for a club which had only existed for five years but they came down to earth with a disappointing bump and were beaten by St Thomas's Hospital in the very first round. Thus Jimmy's experience of Twickenham was short but not especially sweet.

The next year followed the same pattern although he managed to get back to Penzance to face both the Harlequins and Llanelli in two eagerly-awaited fixtures as well as appearing once again against Cardiff.

Older supporters still recall 1952/53 as being a vintage season when the Pirates, under the enthusiastic guidance of Harvey Richards, remained unbeaten until March. The victories included Bath, Rosslyn Park and Blackheath plus an outstanding display at Redruth. Jimmy's contribution could no longer be ignored by Cornwall who drafted him into the second-row for a stirring victory over Gloucestershire at Kingsholm and then for a win over Somerset at Redruth when he scored Cornwall's final try.

After leaving St Luke's, Jimmy did his teaching practice at St Just and then took up a post at Lescudjack and so consequently he could now be counted upon to play a regular part in the club's fortunes. About this time he was often joined in the pack by his younger brother Ron who served the Pirates for several seasons during the late 1950s.

He retained his Cornwall place in the second-row, appearing in all the county matches throughout the next season, and was unlucky not to have made the Cornwall and Devon team to face the All Blacks at Camborne. His ability to play in different positions may have actually counted against him in that the county selectors switched him repeatedly between lock and prop. In fact at one point early in his career he had even turned out for the club as a centre three-quarter.

He had a reputation for keeping himself extremely fit and was an early devotee of weight training decades before the advent of the huge 'gym monkeys' of the modern era. Off the field he kept the Pirate connection in family matters when he married Gaynor – the sister of future Pirates and Cornwall lock David Mann.

Brother-in-law David was also keen on weight training and one day they decided to construct their own makeshift gymnasium in the garden. However the equipment available was somewhat rudimentary and the largest 'barbell' they possessed consisted of two rocks off the beach lashed to the ends of a curtain rail.

In 1955 he was elected to captain the club and was probably at the peak of his career. That season the Pirates fulfilled fifty-five fixtures and Jimmy appeared in all but three of them while again moving around the pack as required. At the end of the season he was back on the sevens circuit leading the Pirates to victory in the inaugural CRFU competition at Camborne.

He then decided to concentrate on being a prop and at last had a settled place in the Cornwall front-row alongside Bonzo Johns and hooker Reg Carter. He was again made captain and led the Pirates on their early season tour of the Scottish Borders but was injured in the first game back at the Mennaye. He reappeared for only a brief spell during the rest of a very frustrating year.

It was back to moving around the pack again but this time his flexibility may have come to his aid. Just before Christmas 1958 Graham Paul had signed for Hull Kingston Rovers in the Rugby League who also needed some mobile forwards who could handle, run and tackle. Jimmy had suffered in the line-out through lack of inches and was not the most punishing prop in the tight but these were not required in rugby league and he seemed ideally suited. Accordingly he joined Graham in East Yorkshire in early 1959.

Things did not turn out quite as well for Jimmy as with his Penzance colleague. He played for a while as a loose forward and was getting into his stride but then smashed his arm severely in a clash at Oldham which necessitated having a plate fitted and effectively finished his rugby career.

He taught in Hull for a period and in due course moved back to the South West to take up a teaching post at a secondary modern in Sidmouth where he became deputy headmaster. He was unfortunately prevented from taking any further part in rugby affairs due to the rigid embargo placed by the Rugby Union on anyone who had moved over to the league code.

Although an occasional visitor, he never returned to settle in Penzance and died in early 2002 at the age of only seventy-one.

# Mike Jenkin

Position: Anywhere in the Backs
Height/Weight: 5'11", 12st 0lbs
Date of Birth: 1930
Died: 1995
Matches: 213
Tries: 73

**Did you know?** Mike once played against Falmouth while still at school partnered by the future *Guardian* rugby writer David Frost

For some people rugby is a life-long love affair and that was certainly true of Mike Jenkin who was once aptly described as a 'rugby romantic'. He possessed a penetrating understanding of the game and an ability to perform anywhere behind the scrum. Indeed he began his Pirates career as a teenage scrum-half and finished it twenty years later captaining the Third XV from full-back having performed equally well at fly-half, centre and on the wing along the way.

He was born in Penzance in 1930 and was the son of Jack Jenkin who ran a local bus company named Duchy Tours and was one of the leading lights in amalgamating the Newlyn and Penzance clubs towards the end of the Second World War. Jack then served as Honorary Treasurer of the newly-formed club during its early years.

Mike started his rugby as a youngster at St Erbyn's and then went on to Kelly College at Tavistock where he excelled in all sports including cricket and athletics. He was still there when he made his debut for the Pirates first team at scrum-half against St Ives in April 1947. Any excitement generated by that event was rather overshadowed by the fact that a huge old battleship named HMS *Warspite* had chosen that particular weekend to break loose and run itself aground upon St Michael's Mount.

At the very end of his schooldays in December 1948 Mike took part in a final Public Schools England Trial. He was actually selected but then subsequently debarred from playing when it was discovered that he had already left school and was consequently technically ineligible. He was nevertheless presented with the relevant tie to mark his achievement.

On leaving school he went off to do his National Service and was commissioned as a Second Lieutenant in the Royal Artillery and enjoyed the opportunity to play plenty of rugby. While stationed in Plymouth he assisted Devonport Services and once played for them against the Pirates. During this time he also made his debut for Cornwall against the British Police in Penzance and scored a try into the bargain.

Once he had completed his time in the army it was time for him to go up to Oxford where he read Modern Languages at Trinity College. He did not get to play in the Varsity match right away as Oxford had three current internationals in their back line but he was nevertheless selected to go on a combined Oxbridge tour of Japan but unfortunately was unable to take up the opportunity. However he captained the Oxford Greyhounds for a period and toured with them in Germany. In December 1952 he finally obtained his Blue on the left wing at Twickenham but Oxford went down by a single point to Cambridge.

On leaving university he came back to Cornwall to take up a trainee teaching post at Truro playing regularly in the centre for both the Pirates and Cornwall and was desperately unlucky not to have been selected to face the All Blacks at Camborne. At the beginning of the 1954/55 season he was elected club captain but at the beginning of October broke his arm and thus was out for the rest of the season.

He felt it was now time to start a business career and so joined Shell as a marketing trainee which enabled him to play for Gloucester. While posted briefly to Shell Centre in London he also turned out at full-back for the Harlequins. He continued to appear intermittently for the Pirates when home on holiday and always brought something special to the side whenever he did so.

In October 1957 he was dramatically recalled by the Cornwall selectors against Gloucestershire at Camborne and celebrated the occasion with the opening try in a dramatic 15-6 victory. The South West Group went to a replay against Devon and once again he gathered a bouncing ball to score what proved to be the winning try. On the strength of this he was compensated for his non-selection against the New Zealanders by playing against Australia at Plymouth.

He then took a full part in the dramatic semi-final win over Lancashire and the snow-flecked epic against Warwickshire in the Final at Coventry. His last match for Cornwall was when he led the team against Surrey early in the following season.

In 1959 he returned to Cornwall to join his old headmaster Rex Carr at St Erbyn's School. For nearly two years he was a First XV regular but played his last match at that level in December 1960. By this time old injuries were beginning to take their toll and senior rugby was ceasing to be the joy it had once been.

Undaunted he then derived great pleasure from running the Third Fifteen where his astute rugby brain more than made up for any reduction in pace. Candidly some of the rugby at that level was fairly basic but the old rugby romantic in him was utterly determined to enjoy every single minute of it.

When his rugby-playing career finally did come to an end he continued to play cricket and ran a regular 'St Erbs' tour each year to Dorset. He coached the Pirates for a while and also served for several seasons as a Cornwall selector. In due course he took over the school at St Erbyn's where he was joined by another ex-Pirate player named Jimmy Reid and continued to give local boys the opportunity to take their first steps in rugby.

Mike always loved to write, whether it was programme notes for the Pirates or as a part-time rugby columnist in the press. He could always be relied upon to produce insightful and balanced articles inevitably laced with his laconic sense of humour.

Unfortunately when still in his early sixties a combination of health and family issues began to weigh heavily upon him and he died prematurely in September 1995 when only sixty-five.

# Matt Jess

Position: Wing
Height/Weight: 5' 11", 13st 7lbs
Date of Birth: 1984
Matches: 66 + 11
Tries: 30

Did you know? When still a teenager Matt helped coach a little boy in the Pirates minis. His name was Jack Nowell, now his wing partner at Exeter Chiefs.

Although born in Coventry, Matt Jess is very much a local Penzance boy hence his nickname of the 'Heamoor Flyer'. His two elder brothers had already played some junior rugby by the time his family initially moved down to St Just and subsequently to settle in Heamoor. His uncle was already based in Cornwall and his cousin had been playing rugby for St Just and so it was there that Matt took his first steps in the game with their mini section.

He moved on to Cape Cornwall School but, on the advice of Adrian Bick, he joined the Pirates junior section in 1997 where he came under the wing of Bez Berryman, Tony Blewett and Lee Mruk. He had an early thrill when Bez, with the help of Sue Holmes, took the boys to play in Kenya. His progress was rapid and he not only made the Cornwall team at the various age levels but came to the notice of Pirates' coach Kevin Moseley who soon saw the potential in the young winger.

Moseley offered Matt a YTS contract while he continued with his studies at Penwith College and trained two evenings a week. He actually played one match for St Just but by this time the Mounts Bay club had been formed and, although still an amateur, he joined them for a season to gain valuable experience and never looked back.

He had been playing and scoring regularly for Mounts Bay when in January 2003 Moseley decided to give him a two match 'taster' with the Pirates. This was a shrewd move by the coach as the team was storming ahead in National League Two and two home games against modest opposition provided an ideal opportunity to see what Matt could produce.

His debut against Kendal went well enough when an open running match was won by a 51-21 margin but frustratingly the next against Doncaster was postponed due to bad weather and it was back to Mounts Bay for Matt for the rest of the season.

The Pirates were duly promoted to what is now the Championship and Matt joined the squad although still on the same YTS basis. He went straight into the team and held his place for the entire season despite a lot of chopping and changing elsewhere. He seemed to have a happy knack of doing well on the big occasions such as in the opening match at ex-Premiership Bristol. A breakaway try against the ultimate Champions Worcester, a hat trick against Manchester and a Powergen Cup match against the mighty Saracens were highlights of his early career.

At the end of the season he played in all Cornwall's championship matches and, following a couple of tries against Middlesex, he had the thrill of going to Canada with the England Counties team where he and the future England man David Strettle took the two wing positions. One match at Edmonton was against a near test-strength Canadian side. He was also called into the England Under 20 squad but never actually got a cap.

His second full season was equally successful with another twenty-five matches and a further eleven tries including two memorable ones at Old Deer Park. He was back representing Cornwall at the end of the season and then went on a second England Counties team to South America to play in front of large and passionate crowds in Buenos Aires, Rosario and Montevideo. Rugby had already taken him a long way from Heamoor.

The year at Kenwyn turned out to be his last with the Pirates. It began well enough but he lost his place just before Christmas and, although he appeared from time to time, he seemed to have lost out to Kevin James, Rhodri McAtee and in particular Richard Welding whenever Jim McKay selected his team.

By the end of the season Matt felt frustrated enough to turn down a contract extension and moved to Gwent Dragons together with Joe Bearman. He returned to play and score against the Pirates in a pre-season friendly but then could not break into the side. He went out on loan to Ebbw Vale but shortly afterwards had his leg broken in a match with Pontypridd.

He had a metal plate removed from his leg and managed to get himself fit that summer but the Dragons had by then released him and thus he had no club. Fortunately the Cornish All Blacks had just been promoted to the Championship and their coaches John Hill and Chris Brown were looking to strengthen their squad. Suddenly his luck seemed to change for the better and, despite the fact that the All Blacks struggled and were immediately relegated, Matt played every minute of every match claiming seventeen tries in the League (including one in both matches against the Pirates) and a further three in the EDF Trophy. This was an extraordinary feat given the fact that his team were usually on the back foot throughout the entire season.

He had been playing for the All Blacks on a part-time basis but, now that they had gone down again, finding a new club was imperative. Fortunately Sale, Northampton and Leeds were all interested but when Peter Drewett of Exeter Chiefs came along Matt did not hesitate to put pen to paper. The Chiefs were then still in the Championship but had a new stadium at Sandy Park and were about to embark upon a serious bid for the Premiership.

This has turned out to be a brilliant move for both club and player. Although the Chiefs were just pipped into second place by Leeds, they made no mistake the following year by outpointing Bristol over the two legs of the first ever Championship play-offs. Matt was fast, hungry and totally committed and both the coaching staff and the supporters soon took him to their hearts.

He has now been a regular at the Chiefs for several years, has made some 200 appearances for them in all competitions and currently stands as the highest try-scorer in

Exeter's admittedly brief Premiership history. He played an important role in the Chiefs winning the LV Cup in 2014 and his burning ambition is to win the Premiership before he retires. Despite the frustration of only missing the playoffs on points difference last season he claimed two tries in the last match against Sale Sharks to take the Man of the Match award.

He takes particular professional satisfaction in the fact that he was part of a close-knit squad which earned the right to play in the Premiership rather than just being signed on for an established club via an agent. Exeter are fortunate in that Rugby Director Rob Baxter clearly values loyalty and commitment and stood by the bulk of the team which won promotion and has since successfully grafted many youngsters into the side from locally-developed talent.

In all this Matt has remained a constant and in early 2015 was awarded a new three-year deal which for a wing just past his thirtieth birthday is a great compliment. Many of those new players have passed through the ranks of the Pirates either as juniors, dual-registered professionals or by simply moving up to the Premiership from another local club. Matt has long held an interest in coaching and has worked with Exeter University for six years. He is currently doing his Level Three coaching badge. He has also helped with the backs at the Pirates on occasion.

He has now become one of the most experienced wings in the Premiership and really relished the European experience especially doing battle in front of the passionate crowds at Montpellier, Stade Français and Clermont Auvergne. Pressed for the most difficult wingers he has faced he plumped for Sitiveni Sivivatu the brilliant New Zealander then at Clermont and, perhaps more surprisingly, Nick Baxter of Birmingham-Solihull.

During his time in Wales Matt met and is now married to a lady from Pembrokeshire and they are settled happily in Exeter. When not actually playing or training for rugby he enjoys a game of squash and a bit of fishing.

# John Kendall-Carpenter CBE

Position: Number 8 / Prop
Height/Weight: 6' 1", 14st 12lbs
Date of Birth: 1925
Died: 1990
Matches: 92
Tries: 17

**Did you know?** John temporarily left an Oxbridge rugby tour of Argentina riding on a mule dressed in a poncho and gaucho hat to try to trace his ancestors.

By any yardstick John McGregor Kendall Kendall-Carpenter was a very remarkable man. He was actually born in Cardiff but by all other criteria he was a man of Penzance when his father became Commander of a local Trinity House vessel.

During the Second World War he attended Truro School but, as a small fresh-faced young boy, he showed no aptitude for rugby whatsoever. His talents appeared to be more on the stage and, according to his school contemporary Harvey Richards, he was frequently given the female roles to play.

John was nevertheless blessed with tireless application and enthusiasm and, having left school, he started at the University of Oxford but almost immediately joined the Fleet Air Arm. He went to train in the USA and, with the benefit of military training and unrationed food, he grew rapidly into the Adonis-like figure of popular memory.

On demobilisation he was back in Penzance and after watching the Pirates' opening match was selected for the second one at Redruth. Waiting to return to his deferred studies at Exeter College, Oxford he worked variously around West Penwith as a farmhand, lumberjack and on the Seven Stones Lightship. At the same time he appeared regularly in the back-row for the club.

Oxford had a glut of top back-row men but they still needed John – so he became a prop. In those days props were expected to push in scrums and puff around between them but not too much else. John however famously brought Twickenham to its feet by saving the Varsity match by downing J. V. Smith the Cambridge and England wing inches from scoring in the corner. Apparently the watching Prime Minister Clement Atlee – an Oxford man – got so excited that he hurled his hat high in the air for it never to be seen again!

During his time at university he toured Argentina with the Combined Oxbridge team winning all their matches and having some great adventures along the way. His reputation thus made, he was soon included in the England team against Ireland in the back-row. England lost but John was again selected for the next match against France but this time as a prop. What he might have made of all the present-day fuss about uncontested scrums would be fascinating to discover. That same season he made the first of numerous appearances for the Barbarians against the East Midlands at Bedford and then joined their traditional Easter tour in Wales.

He nevertheless took his studies very seriously. Having played all four England matches in 1950, he was sounded out for the British Lions tour of New Zealand that summer. His university life had been significantly delayed by the war and, feeling his priority was to complete his degree, he reluctantly declined.

He had been returning regularly to play for the Pirates whenever he could and in that September of 1950 he reputedly played something like sixteen matches in a month. That season he captained Oxford and was then asked to captain England. Injury prevented him from leading his country in the first match at Swansea which may actually have been fortunate as Wales thrashed England. He was promptly recalled to lead the team in Dublin where he was joined by fellow Pirate Ginger Williams who was making his England debut.

The following year he began his distinguished teaching career at Clifton College and decided to join Bath although he continued to play for the Pirates whenever possible. A full season with England was enhanced by three matches against the touring Springboks. He represented Devon and Cornwall at Home Park, Plymouth then England at Twickenham and finally the Barbarians at Cardiff when once again he was switched back to prop-forward.

His appearances for Cornwall had been rather limited by university commitments since his debut at Falmouth in late 1947 but now, playing for Bath, he began to wear the famous black and gold more regularly. Naturally he was asked to lead the team and was described by one notable commentator as being the 'most knowledgeable man playing rugby' which is remarkable given the fact that he only really began to play seriously when he was nearly twenty.

The England captaincy was passed around like a ticking bomb by the capricious England selectors to first Nim Hall and then to the RAF prop Bob Stirling but at least they retained John for the next two years in his preferred place in the back-row. England won the Five Nations in 1953 and at the end of the season he had the unusual honour for a current player of opening the Pirates' new stand which had at last been built just in time for the Coronation.

The All Blacks toured Britain during what turned out to be his last season with England. He led the South West Counties against them at Camborne and though the match was lost he distinguished himself by confronting a group of rowdy supporters who had been jeering and booing the visitors by shouting at them in his best schoolmasterly fashion to 'shut up'. They did.

A titanic struggle at Twickenham resulted in a 5-0 win for New Zealand but victories over Wales and Ireland had left the English in a strong position. Those selectors implausibly then brought in four new caps for the visit to Murrayfield and Carps was among those omitted. He was recalled for the Easter visit to Paris but England lost and his international career was over despite still being only twenty-eight.

He continued with Bath, Cornwall and occasionally the Pirates and left an abiding memory for the Mennaye faithful by blasting over an enormous drop goal from near the touchline one warm September evening. Cornwall meanwhile reached the County Championship semi-finals for the first time since the Second World War but went down to a Middlesex team featuring the new England half-back pairing of Williams and Baker. He was accompanied by fellow England veteran Vic Roberts and their tactical battle with the gifted newcomers was perhaps the last major confrontation of his stellar playing career.

By now he had a senior role at Clifton College and his schooling ambitions and family responsibilities were beginning to take priority so he finished playing in 1956 by going out at the top as the captain of Bath. His achievements in the English public school arena were remarkable in themselves as he was successively Headmaster at Cranbrook, Eastbourne and Wellington effecting many positive changes at each of them. For a while he chaired the influential Headmasters Conference, represented the interests of schools on the Rugby Union and managed an England Schools team to Australia.

In 1980 he was elected President of the Rugby Union as England came within a disputed try of achieving a second Grand Slam and then took the England team back to his old haunts in Argentina. Having served his term, he was elected onto the International Rugby Board. It was then and there that he probably made his biggest contribution of all. The IRB were hopelessly divided upon whether to introduce a World Cup but it was Kendall-Carpenter's willingness to ignore the naysayers and throw in England's vote with the progressives from Wales and the Southern Hemisphere which finally won the day for the now global competition to be first launched in 1987.

He then became one of the leading lights in making all the complicated arrangements for a tournament thousands of miles away and it is related that his welcoming speech at the opening ceremony went on for so long that the television advertisements all had to be re-scheduled. He speeded it up at the conclusion when he presented the Webb Ellis Cup to the victorious Kiwi skipper David Kirk. Needless to say the venture proved a huge success and he was heavily involved in structuring the second and more ambitious one to be held in the UK and France in 1991.

Sadly he died in May 1990 aged only sixty-four a year before that competition began. By then he had received many honours including being made a Bard of the Cornish Gorsedd in 1981 and a CBE by the Queen in 1989. The IRB elected him posthumously into the Rugby Hall of Fame.

# Tom Kessell

Position: Scrum Half
Height/Weight: 6' 0", 13st 4lbs
Date of Birth: 1990
Matches: 74 + 37
Tries: 30

Did you know? While most Pirate supporters refer to Tom affectionately as Kess he was christened Mr Burns by Blair Cowan after the character in *The Simpsons*.

Thomas Treeve Kessell was born in Truro and spent his early childhood in Hayle where his father had worked at the St Ivel creamery and played rugby in the centre for the Hayle club. When he was only five he and his twin brother began mini rugby at the Pirates.

Soon afterwards the family moved to Shepton Mallet in Somerset where he joined the minis at Wells RFC. He also played football for Shepton Mallet Juniors but had already settled as a scrum-half at rugby and was by then developing his bullet-like passing skills. In 2001 he progressed to Whitstone School and also began travelling to play for the youngsters at Bath where the coaching was at a higher level. Having gained selection for the local Mendip area team, he represented Somerset at Under 16 and Under 17 level while captaining his school.

In 2007 he made his first entry into senior rugby joining Bridgwater during the mid-season and making a number of appearances for the club who were then in National III South. At this time he was beginning an apprenticeship for the building trade and still training with Bath Colts.

One of his coaches had been the ex-England forward Ben Sturnham who went off to manage Newbury in 2008 and soon signed Tom on a part-time basis. At that time Newbury were a very useful Championship team with financial backing from Vodafone. By coincidence Tom's debut entailed coming off the bench against the Pirates at Camborne to be chased around the park by Chris Morgan who was playing his first game back at the Pirates – having himself just left Newbury. Rugby is indeed a small world.

He had about twelve Championship matches for Newbury including starting and scoring against Coventry. That season was particularly brutal as the RFU in their infinite wisdom decided to reduce the Championship from sixteen to a mere twelve teams with the result that five teams were doomed to be relegated and unfortunately this included Newbury. Vodafone cancelled their sponsorship and that fine community rugby club has never fully recovered.

Tom then decided to give up the idea of working in the building trade and concentrate on gaining a full-time rugby contract. He had contact with several clubs including Sale and the Cornish Pirates but they already had Gavin Cattle returning from Llanelli Scarlets and had also just signed James Doherty from Wharfedale.

If he could not yet get back to Cornwall, he did make it down as far as Plymouth and signed for Albion. When Tom went along for his try-out with Albion, their rugby director Graham Dawe had forgotten he was coming and was just rushing out to attend a funeral. However, an hour later Dawe was back out on the Brickfields pitch still in his dark suit and black tie taking passes and box-kicks from Tom and then promptly signed him up.

He had to bide his time for a while as Dawe already had two scrum-halves in Ruaridh Cushion and Josh Lewsey's brother Ed available. Nevertheless Tom came off the bench in a televised play-off match at Brickfields against the Pirates and did well. By the end of his second season he had made the position his own and achieved fifteen successive starts in the spring of 2011.

Tom also got a call to play for Devon and actually appeared against Cornwall which must have seemed strange for a lad from Hayle. After a particularly good display against Hertfordshire he was selected for the English Counties team to tour Canada and appeared in Toronto, Vancouver and St John's in Newfoundland.

In that second season he had also played against the Pirates at the Mennaye and had once again impressed Chris Stirling and Harvey Biljon. Although Albion offered him a new contract, he decided to come to Penzance not least for the opportunity of learning the finer nuances of scrum-half play from Gavin Cattle and Biljon.

Indeed the Pirates had made something of a habit of signing Albion players and while at Brickfields Tom had partnered Kieran Hallett as well as appearing with Kyle Marriott, Matt Hopper, Aaron Carpenter and Ben Mercer. The Pirates had decided to deepen the squad and employ three scrum-halves for the first time. He arrived as probably the logical third choice behind the self-same Cattle and Doherty and for the first couple of months only got to start in the B & I cup wins over Bristol and Albion where he celebrated by scoring against his old team on his first return to Brickfields. He also had a trip to Clonmel in Ireland to take on the massively experienced Ireland scrum-half Peter Stringer who was in the Munster team that day.

He got his first Championship start in a win over London Scottish and, by the second half of the season, had supplanted Doherty as the heir apparent to the illustrious Cattle. He came on to replace his skipper during the latter period of the home semi-final thrashing of Bristol when the Pirates had run riot and then appeared again as a replacement in both legs of the Championship Final with London Welsh.

That autumn he displaced Cattle for the first time at Bristol and again the following week for the visit of Newcastle Falcons. The contrast between the styles of the two men was intriguing for Pirates supporters. The vastly more experienced Cattle was still far ahead in terms of game management, still had the best left-footed box kick in the Championship and could perform apparent miracles behind a retreating pack. Tom on the other hand had a superb fast flat pass and an explosive break which was soon to bring him a host of tries. Furthermore under Biljon's prompting and Cattle's example his kicking had improved significantly.

The Pirates opened his third season by overturning Bristol at neutral Exeter and Tom, having again come off the bench, was central to directing a valiant defensive effort. Soon afterwards he at last began to be selected as first choice for most key matches and was starting to score regularly including a spell of six tries in just four Championship matches during November. By then he had become noticeably more assertive on the field and it was no surprise when he was asked to captain the team in Chris Morgan's absence for the last two matches of the season at Bedford and Leeds.

His fourth and final year saw him not only as the clear first choice scrum-half but also a key leader beside Morgan in a relatively inexperienced squad. That autumn he was recognised with selection for the Championship team which defeated Canada at Worcester and by this time it was clear that a few Premiership clubs would be bidding for his signature. He was also placed in the Championship Dream Team.

After being recommended by ex-England full-back Dusty Hare and having had a long discussion with Northampton's backs coach Alex King, Tom finally decided to join the Saints. Furthermore he joined Bristol on a short-term loan deal to assist with their promotion battle with Worcester Warriors. They fell agonisingly at that final hurdle and one TV pundit felt strongly that he should have been used at the expense of Bristol's veteran captain Dwayne Peel.

As a youngster Tom's favourite player was Matt Dawson – the brilliant scrum half for both Northampton and England – and now he can contemplate the opportunity to follow in his old hero's footsteps.

# Gerald Luke

Position: Centre
Height/Weight: 5' 9", 13st 10 lbs
Date of Birth: 1934
Matches: 378
Tries: 140

**Did you know?** Aged only fifteen Gerald is still considered to be the youngest player ever to have appeared in the Pirates' First XV when he and Jim Matthews (who was only slightly older) made their debuts together in 1950.

Gerald Gruzelier Luke was another teenage rugby prodigy. He was born in Mousehole as a member of an extended rugby-loving family in that his grandfather had been Treasurer of Penzance RFC while his cousins Peter, Mike and Terry Luke all played for the Pirates while other cousins are the extensive rugby-playing Mungles family from Hayle.

He started in the game while attending Penzance Grammar School which did not have a rugby team at the time but he nevertheless soon found his way towards the Pirates.

Gerald was only thirteen and merely watched for a while but soon showed what he could do in the club Colts team and then with Mounts Bay from the tender age of fourteen. In 1949 both he and his school friend Jim Matthews played for England Under 15s. A photograph of the two of them proudly wearing their white England shirts standing alongside John Kendall-Carpenter (who had gained his first full 'cap' that same season) hung prominently in the school assembly hall for years. They also gained England honours at Youth and ATC level.

In April 1950 the young duo made their senior debuts together against Gloucester when he lined up in the centre alongside the experienced Dave Porritt. The following season both of them were regulars in the team and Gerald scored the first of his huge total of tries against Blackheath. He was by now impressing onlookers with his aggressive running, deceptive dummy, side-step and, for such a young boy, a front-on tackle which would flatten a rogue elephant. He was primarily a centre but, with the Pirates able to call upon Ginger Williams and Mike Terry for those positions, he showed that he could also perform equally well on the wing. Indeed it was the aggressive Terry who largely inspired Gerald in his tackling.

He was then called up for National Service in the RAOC where he spent two years at Bramley in Hampshire getting bored but relieving it with playing a good standard of rugby for Aldershot Services and county rugby, somewhat bizarrely, not for Cornwall but for Hampshire. He had already made nearly seventy first team appearances for the Pirates but, for the next few seasons, he was only seen when home on leave or on holiday from college. He returned to Penzance several times including on one notable occasion when he scored a brilliant try against the Pirates for Aldershot Services.

In January 1955 Cornwall had won the South Western Group and faced a quarter-final with Berkshire at Redruth. The selectors turned to Gerald and he made his debut on the wing and celebrated the occasion with two tries. Cornwall won decisively but then Middlesex came to town for the first of Gerald's four county semi-finals with a team packed with international players. He found himself directly facing the burly Ted Woodward who, if not of Jonah Lomu proportions, was nevertheless then considered to be the most intimidating winger in European rugby.

He survived the ordeal well enough but sadly Cornwall did not and the chance of a County Championship disappeared in the February murk. Gerald however had made himself a fixture in the county team and was to go on to forty matches for Cornwall before he finished.

Having left the army, he decided upon a teaching career and, for a young rugby star in Cornwall, there was only one place to go and that was St Luke's College in Exeter where several Pirates including Jimmy Jenkin, Alvin Williams and Johnny Thomas had already shown their mettle.

During his time there he played under the inspired captaincy of Welsh flanker Brian Sparks and alongside the brilliant Benny Jones from Pontypool. He found himself opposing the Pirates again and also played a major role in St Luke's winning the prestigious Middlesex Sevens against London Welsh at Twickenham in 1957. The Londoners had a bevy of Welsh internationals but the students' superior pace and fitness won the day.

The following year brought further progress. Cornwall battled through to the County Championship final at Coventry having disposed of Lancashire in a titanic struggle at Redruth when Gerald eclipsed the new England centre Malcolm Phillips.

The final was a glorious, if chastening, experience played in a minor snowstorm where the Cornwall midfield of Paul, Hosen and Gerald repeatedly threatened while playing into the elements but the intimidating Warwickshire pack slowly gained the upper hand and finally won the day. A fortnight earlier he had played for the South West Counties which drew with Australia at Home Park in Plymouth.

Having graduated from St Luke's, he nearly joined Bedford with a teaching job promised at Bedford School. However, due to his father's death, he decided to return to the family in Cornwall and became the head of Physical Education at the newly-opened Heamoor Secondary school and this was to be his job for the rest of his playing career and beyond.

Gaining the attention of national selectors while based in Cornwall is always a tough thing to do. Nevertheless his consistent displays earned him a brief chance in December 1959 in the senior side for the first England Trial which was held at the unlikely venue of Banbury. He probably should not have turned out as he was suffering from a heavy blow on the leg which had not responded to treatment and, after another knock, was effectively crippled and had to limp off at half-time. His team won but sadly Gerald was not called upon again.

By then an established and experienced centre in his prime, he reeled off countless fine displays for the Pirates. He was by now fast, fit, tigerishly competitive and hard as nails.

Further county semi-finals were reached against Surrey at Twickenham in 1960 and Warwickshire back at Coventry in 1962 but again the Cornish failed to make it to the final.

For the season 1962/63 he was elected captain of one of the strongest units the Pirates ever fielded during their amateur days. He could call upon a backs unit which included Peter Michell, Johnny Thomas, Tony Stevenson, Owen Barnes, Geoff Mungles and occasionally Jimmy Glover and he made the most of it. The team played spectacular rugby and had an unbeaten run of over twenty matches between December and Easter when they were finally downed only after a titanic struggle with the Wasps.

The next season saw his last appearances for Cornwall but, although his glory days were now probably behind him, he continued to be a rock in the Pirates' line-up. The blistering pace may have lost half a yard but his timing of a pass, thunderous defence and tactical nous were very much self-evident. He then stopped playing for a period and slipped easily into becoming the Pirates' very first coach but in September 1966 he resumed playing.

After nearly 400 matches for the Pirates, despite long periods away in the army and at college, at the age of thirty-four he finally called it a day. Almost his very last act in the Pirates first team was to save a match against Esher and gain a daw with a late drop goal – something he had practically never attempted before.

After many years teaching at Heamoor he managed his wife's family laundry business and is now retired and living in Gulval where he takes great pride in the careers of his daughter and two sons one of whom, Cordell, has had a distinguished and highly active service career in the army.

He remains a great believer in the constructive use of possession, continuity and movement as the essence of rugby but confesses to finding quite a lot of current tactics in the modern professional game rather too 'safety first' and just a bit sterile.

# Vili Ma'asi

Position: Hooker/Flanker
Height/Weight: 5' 10", 16st 8lbs
Date of Birth: 1975
Matches: 101 + 28
Tries: 24

**Did you know? Vili is one of a family of six rugby playing brothers.**

The Kingdom of Tonga is a group of over a hundred islands and has a population of a mere 100,000 which makes it significantly smaller than Cornwall. It was once known as the Friendly Islands with good reason and the people in that tiny country have built up a reputation for close family bonds, a deep Christian faith and an abiding love of rugby football in all its various forms – union, league, tens and sevens.

It was in this environment that Viliami Ma'asi was born into a large family at a place called Tofoa which is just outside the capital of Nuku'alofa. He started to play at the age of twelve and performed in the back-row which continued to be his secondary position throughout his career at the Pirates. He went to a local rugby-playing catholic school and then in 1992 went on for a further year at Tonga College where he studied science. He actually stopped playing for two years but was persuaded by a friend to take it up again and joined a local club named Fasi Ma'ufanga where he continued to play for the next six years.

He made a rapid impact and in 1996 was picked to represent Tonga in the ten-a-side version of the game which is extremely popular in the Pacific Rim area. A year later he was chosen to visit Europe with the Tongan team and made his international debut as hooker against Wales at Swansea where he found himself facing Barry Williams fresh from a Lions tour of South Africa. Tonga were soundly beaten but Vili had performed well and was clearly making his mark.

The Tongans had opened their tour against a President's team at Redruth and so when Vili came to sign for the Pirates four years later he already knew a little about Cornwall.

Although he did not make the squad for the 1999 World Cup, he returned to the UK in 2001 to again face Wales at the Millennium Stadium and then came on as a replacement against Scotland at Murrayfield. At the end of that short tour Vili decided to stay on and see if he could find a club which would give him a professional contract. The season was by then half over and most clubs already had their full complement of players so it was not going to be easy.

Vili stayed with a Tongan teammate named Epi Taione who was then playing for Newcastle. Taione was a massive winger who later gained a certain harmless notoriety by attempting to change his name by deed poll to Paddy Power to try to boost his earning potential. Pirates coach Kevin Moseley was interested and Vili thus arrived in Penzance just before Christmas 2001.

The warmth of life back in Tonga, where he had already started a family, must have seemed a very long way away but, in Nat Saumi and Lakalaka Waqanivere, he found two teammates from approximately the same part of the world and he settled in quickly.

After a brief initial appearance as a replacement against Westcombe Park, he made a dynamic debut against Redruth having captured the hooking berth from Danny Clackwothy. The Pirates won promotion from National III and he was by then a permanent fixture in the team.

The following season in National II he had more competition for his hooking position from the ex-Albion man James Owen but, as Vili was much too talented to be omitted, Moseley moved him back to flank-forward. He had actually captained the side on a couple of occasions in the absence of Joe Bearman and with the fiery Kevin Penrose, Waqanivere, Ali Durant and Richard Carroll all vying for places in the back-row, they were far too strong for most National II opponents as a second promotion was achieved at a canter.

He was away as a hooker on World Cup duty in Australia for the early part of the Pirates' first Championship season appearing against Italy, Wales, New Zealand and Canada. Tonga lost all four matches but he nevertheless became the first man to take part in a World Cup competition while currently a Pirate. In all Vili played some thirty-two times for Tonga throughout his career.

He returned to Cornwall in time to play in the big cup tie with the Saracens – once again reverting to being a flanker – but the team were having a torrid time and suffering a string of heavy defeats. After one such thrashing at Plymouth Albion, the Pirates signed the bulky Dan Farini into their back row and Vili was left out for a few weeks only to return as a hooker for a victory over Otley. He was then in the side for the rest of the season and remained as a hooker for the rest of his career.

Over the next two years the Pirates' squad was strengthened significantly and two other hookers were signed in Nick Makin from Newcastle and Peter Ince from Orrell. Competition was fierce and each had their particular strengths but Vili's bullock-like charges and thunderous tackles left Pirates fans in no doubt as to who was their particular favourite. His warm personality and obvious devotion to his young family also marked him out for a special place in their affections.

His last season was undoubtedly his best and coincided with the team moving its home fixtures to Camborne. His long term prop-forwards, Seal and Paver had now been joined in the front-row stakes by the twenty-stone Cornishman Sam Heard who many saw as a young man with a big future. Vili had always scored his fair share of tries but when the EDF competition came along he surpassed himself by embarking upon a memorable run of getting one in every round.

Having sat out the first match with Moseley, he claimed the first in the snowy epic at Leeds, then another in the thriller at Doncaster, yet another in the semi-final against Albion at Camborne and finally the winner at Twickenham itself. During those four breathless cup ties the Pirates only scored five tries in total – and Vili had claimed four of them.

Vili's performance at Leeds must have made them sit up and take notice as, by the end of the season, both he and Alberto di Bernardo were on their way to Yorkshire. Leeds had just secured promotion to the Premiership and both men secured regular places throughout the season with Vili making sixteen starts in the League plus several more from the bench. In his second match he came on as a second-half replacement to score one of his trademark tries against the Harlequins and repeated this against Calvisano in the European Challenge Cup. Leeds suffered relegation in that first season but bounced back again the following year and Vili continued to feature in most of the match day squads although in his third and final year he often had to cover for Andy Titterall.

In the summer of 2011 he moved to London Welsh and returned with them to the Mennaye early in the season and once again in the play-off semi-finals. He was to meet the Pirates for one last time when he came on in the next season's final as a replacement at Oxford's Kassam Stadium as the Dragons made it to the Premiership for the very first time.

In recent times he has been captain and player/coach at Ampthill RFC in Bedfordshire which he recently led to promotion from National II South. The Ma'asi genes continue to flourish in the sport as Vili's seventeen-year-old son is already a very promising centre.

# Rhodri McAtee

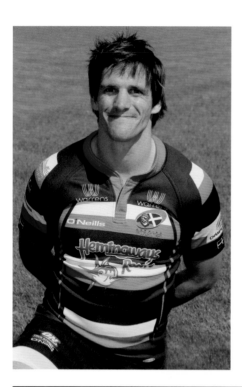

Position: Utility Back
Height/Weight: 5' 10", 13st 0lbs
Date of Birth: 1984
Matches: 144 + 47
Tries: 64

Did you know? On sevens duty with Wales in the dangerous city of Tbilisi in Georgia Rhodri and his team were confined to a vile hotel which a week later was blown up by Russian insurgents.

Rhodri Iain McAtee was born in Newport into a rugby-mad family environment. His father had played a few times for Newport and more regularly for the local team Newport H.S.O.B. They moved to Camberley in Surrey with his father's job and where his mother also worked at Sandhurst Military College. Indeed his father continued playing rugby after having moved to Switzerland and only finished at the age of fifty-five.

Both Rhodri and his sister were rugby players and she played women's rugby for South East England. Rhodri began at Camberley at the age of four and went all the way through the boys and youth teams up to Under 18s apart from a spell with London Welsh Colts.

At this stage his position was scrum-half where his speed and distribution skills were best seen and allowed him to be constantly involved in the game. Representative rugby followed with Surrey Clubs and then England at Under 18 level when he played in a school World Cup competition in France alongside England star James Haskell.

The coach to England Schools had moved to manage the Worcester Academy and was instrumental in taking Rhodri on to the next stage. Initially he was a part-timer studying at Worcester University but after a year he signed a full-time contract and left college life. Although Worcester was still a National I (Championship) club it was highly ambitious and already had a Premiership style coaching staff which included the England veteran Nigel Redman and analyst Andy Keast.

He made eighteen first team appearances for the Warriors including playing and scoring against the Pirates at Sixways and later coming off the bench in the return at the Mennaye. However in May he was told that he was being released.

Several clubs were contacted and a call was put through to Kevin Moseley who was then the Head Coach at the Pirates. Rhodri did not have a driving licence and thus turned up on Penzance station clutching the proverbial suitcase. He was unlikely to be lonely however as the Pirates had signed four players from the Warriors namely Duncan Marray, Wes Davies, Matt Evans and Rhodri himself.

Joining the Pirates as a scrum-half, he found that the current incumbent was the now Exeter staff coach Ricky Pellow. Cornishman Pellow was experienced and tough with an imaginative and accurate service while his young rival was a totally different type of player as he darted, swerved and chip-kicked his way through matches.

His debut was off the bench during a relatively easy pre-season friendly at Launceston together with a starting place against Cross Keys. This was followed with a much tougher League baptism at home against Bristol. He celebrated with a try but the Pirates lost and suddenly a new scrum-half rival appeared on the scene. His name was Gavin Cattle.

Cattle took his place but, following an early cup exit at Coventry, Rhodri came back for a storming win at London Welsh when he raced away for a thrilling 50-metre individual try and kept the scrum-half shirt for the next two months. When Cattle returned it was time for the new coach Jim McKay to exploit Rhodri's innate flexibility and by the end of the season he was back in the team – but now in his main future Pirate position on the wing. It was at this time that he decided to throw in his lot with Wales, the land of his birth, and was capped at Under 21 level.

His second season was repeatedly interrupted by injuries including being taken off in the first minute of the opening fixture at Doncaster. In the return fixture at Kenwyn a few months later McKay picked him at full-back and he responded with a dazzling hat-trick. One week later he was selected to do the same against Newbury but once again was to be taken off injured.

By now he had become a noted exponent of the seven-a-side game and had stood out like a beacon for the Pirates at competitions at Henley and in Kenya. He was soon called into the Wales squad and played all over the world on sevens duty culminating in them winning the World Sevens title in 2009. Rhodri is probably the most travelled rugby player to have been with the Pirates having played the game in Japan, Australia, New Zealand, USA, South Africa, Dubai, Hong Kong, Croatia, Georgia and the Cayman Islands as well as all over Europe and the British Isles.

For the next few seasons he was usually a regular in the back line and yearned to be constantly in the action. He sometimes found being stuck out on the wing in horrible weather rather frustrating but seized every opportunity to become involved. In 2007 he started in every round of the EDF Trophy including the Twickenham triumph over Exeter. The next season saw him lining up against Northampton and Leicester and getting a brace of tries against Plymouth Albion.

Other personal highlights included the B & I Cup Final at Camborne in 2010 against Munster when he crashed over in the corner to claim what turned out to be the deciding try and win the trophy. A further one was the Championship playoffs against his old club Worcester and it was in yet another playoff final that he made his last appearance for the

Pirates at the Kassam Stadium in Oxford against London Welsh. During this time he was selected for the Barbarians against the Combined Services at Devonport alongside team colleague Rhys Jones.

After eight seasons with the Pirates his leaving was somewhat shrouded in disappointment – not only to Rhodri himself but to his small army of admirers who had taken him to their hearts due to his electric zig-zag running and large number of spectacular tries. Their hearts had also gone out both to him and Hannah his young Cornish wife when they suffered a personal tragedy when their little infant daughter Emilie had died after only three months of life.

As a player from the Welsh Sevens team, Rhodri was registered as a non-English Qualified Player under the new rules adopted by the Rugby Football Union. This placed Rhodri at a disadvantage when the new retained lists were drawn up. He had set his heart on reaching the magic 200 appearances which is a key professional milestone and this was now to elude him. The EQP rules are there for a purpose but it does seem odd when Kiwis, South Africans and Samoans can somehow play for England.

By now he had commenced further study and was looking to play as a part-time professional and, while offers from France were considered, he opted to do the long commute from his home in Goldsithney near Penzance to Plymouth to play and train for the Albion. After a generally successful season as a full-back he again fell foul of the EQP rules and his time at Championship level appeared to be over.

He continued to play in numerous sevens competitions around the UK and Europe and has since appeared as an amateur for Redruth usually in his declared favourite position of fly-half which curiously was a job he was practically never asked to perform while at the Pirates.

Settled in Cornwall, he now works in the property letting business in Penzance and is enjoying the odd game of football whenever he gets the chance.

# Laurie McGlone

Position: Number 8/Lock
Height/Weight: 6'3", 18st 10lbs
Date of Birth: 1979
Matches: 121 + 20
Tries: 11

**Did you know?** Laurie was brought up in such a remote area of the extreme north of New Zealand that he was seven years old before they had electricity.

New Zealander Laurie McGlone was born and raised near the town of Kaitaia which is at the extreme northern tip of North Island and as such could almost be described as the John O'Groats of New Zealand. Unlike the tip of Scotland it has a warm climate and Laurie's father was a fisherman who worked with his own boat. His father, brother and sister had also played rugby but injury had curtailed his father's ambitions in the sport by the age of twenty-one. The sea inevitably played a large part in young Laurie's life and he still has a deep affection for sailing.

His own introduction to rugby came when All Black legend Sid Going came to talk to the children at his school. As a youngster he played for a club called Eastern United and also for Kaitaia itself. Given that the nearest town of any size is Whangarei and that is over 100 miles south it must have all taken place in quite a close-knit community.

In his teens he went off to school at Nelson in South Island and played for the Nelson's Bay area teams at Under 16 and Under 18 levels. It was then time to go to university and he went right down to Dunedin in Otago to study land surveying. This was a five year course and in his case included the surveying of vineyards – a profession he may yet return to once his rugby days are over.

Dunedin is a passionate rugby city (its old stadium Carisbrook used to be known as the 'house of pain') and, having played for Otago Under 18, he began to stand out in the university team. Indeed he did so well that he went to Sydney to represent the New Zealand universities against their Australian counterparts.

Once graduated, he moved to Blenheim to work as a surveyor and played his rugby for Moutere RFC and also captained the local regional team known as the Marlborough Red Devils who were coached by another legendary All Black called Alex 'Grizz' Wyllie. Their big local rivals were Nelson's Bay whose key Number 8 was Mark Bright who was later to play for Redruth and London Scottish. Little did they realise as they battled away that they would be doing it all over again a decade later on the other side of the world.

Like most young Kiwis, Laurie wanted to see a bit of the world and rugby was always going to be a passport. One of his previous coaches, Murray Henderson, had spent time in Japan but had by then moved on to work in Italy. In 2006 he signed Laurie to come and play for Parma where he stayed for a season. He liked Italy but the rugby was extremely sterile and, not speaking Italian, he had to rely upon an interpreter. This turned out to be his direct rival for the same back-row position on the team. He soon discovered that his 'interpreter' was taking in whatever the Italian forwards' coach was demanding and then relaying the complete opposite to an uncomprehending Laurie. It was not a situation destined for success!

Henderson then became coach at Coventry and this was Laurie's next stop. Coventry had much going for them as they were a well-established rugby city with a new ground and some good players but unfortunately a profligate owner led them rapidly into financial distress. Laurie had been playing alongside other future Pirates Carl Rimmer, Ian Nimmo and Rudi Brits and they all found themselves out on the streets with buckets collecting money in a desperate attempt to keep the club alive.

Another Pirate Brett Davey had also been at Coventry as a backs coach and it was through that connection that Laurie made his way to Cornwall in 2009. By the time he reached Penzance Davey had moved on but Laurie found himself working for Chris Stirling – another man from his homeland.

He marked his debut in a pre-season win over Cardiff with a try and soon became a fixture in the pack alternating between his favoured position of Number 8 and lock where he could perform equally well. Immensely strong, fit and hard but invariably scrupulously fair he soon established himself as a bit of a cult figure with supporters.

In his first season he missed very few matches playing in all the play-off games as well as in all the latter games in the B & I cup run and was at the core of the pack which carried off the trophy in the final itself. In his second he seemed to get even better. The team had progressed significantly from the previous year and stormed to the Championship final with Worcester and once again Laurie was invariably in the thick of all the action.

He has great upper body strength enabling him to be a massive presence in mauls and breakdowns and is very hard to shift once bridged over the ball. This innate strength also makes him a formidable scrummager. Though no slouch he is not especially fast and he is used as much as a lifter as a jumper in line-outs but his tackle rates and catch-and-drives from re-starts are legendary.

Over the next four years he kept churning out fine performances week after week and he was again at centre stage when the Pirates reached their second Championship final with London Welsh. In the autumn of 2012 Ian Davies asked him to lead the team in Cattle's absence and he did a fine job in his understated way winning two and drawing one of the three matches when he was at the helm.

Perhaps one of his best games in recent years was a televised match with Bristol at Sandy Park in Exeter when the Pirates defended wave after wave of frantic assaults upon their line. If one wanted to make an analogy with the defence of the Alamo then for Jim Bowie you could read Laurie McGlone.

In the past couple of seasons he has inevitably picked up a few more injuries but has fought his way doggedly back to full fitness each time. The Pirates have also needed to introduce a considerable number of young forwards into the squad and Laurie has been invaluable as a mentor, role model and occasional 'minder' for each of them. Late last season he, together with Chris Morgan, was honoured with selection for the Barbarians in a special match against Heriots in Edinburgh.

He is now very much a family man and the proud father of little twins. West Cornwall bears more than a passing resemblance to the extremes of North Auckland where he grew up and he really enjoys being back by the sea.

# Peter Michell

Position: Scrum Half
Height/Weight: 5' 9", 12st 0lbs
Date of Birth: 1933
Matches: 507
Tries: 46

Did you know? Peter played in his first Cornwall county match playing for the opposition against Cornwall.

Peter James Bennett Michell was born in Penzance and grew up in a family firm of jewellers started by his grandfather over a hundred years ago. He got his first taste of rugby at St Erbyn's school which has given birth to the rugby careers of generations of Pirates. He then followed in his father's footsteps to Wycliffe College in Gloucestershire where his rugby developed quickly and soon found himself in the Cornwall Schools team when home on holiday. He was already settled as a scrum-half where he gained selection for an England Schools trial at Gloucester.

Because he was away at school, Peter played very little rugby for the Colts or Mounts Bay. When he was called up at short notice for his first senior match against the Civil Service the gateman failed to recognise the curly-haired young lad who was still at school and he had to hand over sixpence just to get in. Two weeks later he underwent a much sterner test when he faced up to Swansea who gave the Pirates a sound beating.

The Pirates were led by their current scrum-half, Cornwall player and war hero Vivian 'Tinker' Taylor who was re-elected as captain for the following year. Peter got a couple of opportunities over Christmas but by the following Easter he finally displaced the older man and for the next fifteen years the first team position was essentially his own apart from his time away on National Service.

This was deferred for two years while he served his apprenticeship in the jewellery business and during this period he was paired with the highly experienced Harvey Richards and the two of them together enjoyed perhaps the most glorious period in amateur Pirates history. Their fixtures included Harlequins, Cardiff, Gloucester, Wasps and Blackheath as well as all the top West Country clubs. Despite this in season 1952/53 Richards led them unbeaten until mid-March and Peter hardly missed a match over those two seasons.

All this changed when he was finally called up to the Royal Artillery to fulfil his National Service obligations where he discovered he thoroughly enjoyed the army life and began to undergo training to be an officer. He was posted to Eaton Hall in Cheshire where he took part in an eagerly anticipated Royal Artillery vs Royal Engineers match which also featured the budding Redruth hero Bonzo Johns.

By declaring he would continue to serve the new young Queen in the Territorials after his initial year was over he was able to transfer to the Duke of Cornwall's Light Infantry and soon found himself in the then colony of sunny Jamaica. There were certainly far worse places to be posted.

During his army service he had played plenty of rugby for the Regiment, the Royal Artillery and gained his Inter-Services cap against the Royal Navy at Twickenham. He had also managed to be released to play for Cornwall and made his debut in October 1953 against Gloucestershire at Redruth. Curiously he had actually turned out against Cornwall just a few weeks earlier partnering the famous Dr Jack Matthews for Dai Gent's XV at Falmouth.

However he had not been seen in a Pirates shirt for two years when he ran out against Pontypridd to open the 1955/56 season but success came his way almost immediately. Many of the post-war stars such as Mike Terry, Kendall-Carpenter, Richards and Ginger Williams had faded from the scene but he had found an exciting new half-back partner in another of Penzance's returning servicemen – Graham Paul.

In his first season back he reclaimed his Cornwall place, helped win the inaugural Cornish Sevens and the following year was made the Pirates captain. This was followed by a momentous year for rugby in Cornwall when he and his partner Paul plus other colleagues in Gerald Luke, Mike Jenkin and Alvin Williams starred in a glorious run to the Final with Warwickshire at Coventry. Cornwall lost the match but Peter had clearly outshone his opposite number who was the prodigious goal-kicker George Cole.

Peter lost his county place briefly to Penryn's Ray Plummer after Cornwall's disappointing display against Somerset in the first-ever Championship match held at Penzance. He bounced back the following year to lead both the Pirates and Cornwall onto higher things when Cornwall reached another semi-final with Surrey at Twickenham and his powerful Pirates team claimed several notable victims including Saracens and Cardiff.

In December 1960 a highlight of his career was leading a combined South West Counties team against Avril Malan's Springboks at Camborne. The visitors had a somewhat dour reputation but in a thrilling match the Counties scored three tries and with better goal-kicking might have given the Boks a real scare.

Various rugby scribes had intimated that he might be considered by the England selectors but, with the charismatic Dicky Jeeps firmly in control of the England berth, no call even for a trial was forthcoming. Many lesser performers had also been honoured by the Barbarians but in both cases he was ignored as have so many fine players from Cornwall before and since.

Despite this, he was instrumental in Cornwall reaching yet another county semi-final in 1962 and two years later he partnered Richard Sharp for the South West vs New Zealand at Exeter. The All Blacks proved far too strong and, behind a pack which was gasping for air long before the finish, both he and Sharp had a difficult afternoon.

Having led the Pirates for a then record third time, his last three seasons coincided with a slow but inexorable downturn in the club's fortunes. By this time he was partnering the highly-talented young Roger Pascoe and prompted by the older man's shrewd service young 'Paco' began to demonstrate his precocious talent. Indeed Peter's skill, experience and dogged determination in the face of adversity were priceless assets in a team which often struggled.

As a player he was always very much a gentleman who was never given to histrionics on the field but was nevertheless pragmatic, tough-minded and highly competitive. That pragmatism occasionally opened him up to criticism from some rugby followers in that he often closed games down by working the touchlines with his trusty left foot under the laws prevailing at that time.

Whereas it is possibly true that there were certain times when a game might have been won by a wider margin had he been more expansive, there were many more occasions when he pulled his team through to a narrow victory having been given a torrid time up front. That reliable left boot also claimed a very large number of drop-goals at critical moments and he still holds the club record for that particular form of scoring.

Throughout his career he was able to forge several notable half-back partnerships. This began with two older and more experienced men in Harvey Richards and – to a lesser extent – Harry Oliver of St Ives. On his return from service overseas he enjoyed the opportunity to link up with Graham Paul and the nimble and quick-witted Johnny Thomas to be followed by Richard Sharp who coincidentally is his cousin. Sharp, who older rugby followers will recall fondly as the 'Prince of the Outside Break', always insisted upon a very fast service from his inside partner which Peter was always willing and able to provide.

Finally he was able to help the young and talented Roger Pascoe to find his feet in the game. Those six men were all blessed with high ability but very different in their requirements. They all owed a considerable debt to not only the service but also the protection Peter was able to provide for them.

Having retired from rugby after well over 500 matches for the Pirates and a further sixty for Cornwall, he continued with the family business and served both as a Major in the Territorial Army and as a magistrate for thirty years. He also received an award at Buckingham Palace from Prince Philip for his many years of work for the Playing Fields Association.

In recent years he took on the duties as President of the Cornwall Rugby Football Union.

# Chris Morgan

Position: Flanker
Height/Weight: 6' 2", 16st 10lbs
Date of Birth: 1981
Matches: 167 + 27
Tries: 16

**Did you know? Chris was taken along to ballet lessons as a youngster.**

Chris Morgan was born in Bristol but brought up just down the coast at Burnham-on-Sea from where his family ran a pub back in Bristol. His father had principally been a sprinter but had also played some rugby and therefore Chris naturally made his way to the minis at Burnham RFC.

When he was thirteen he went to Kings Wessex in Cheddar which was a strong rugby school and he was soon playing for them on Wednesday afternoons and for his club at weekends. He did well enough for Somerset Schools to make the South West teams and to get into the England Trials but did even better with the England Under 18 Club's team – getting capped in a tournament at Murrayfield in a team which included the future Pirate Paul Devlin.

He was given a rugby-based scholarship to Millfield where he stayed for two years doing his A Levels and gained Under 18 England caps against Wales, Ireland and France. By this time he had been approached by Gloucester Academy but decided to stay closer to home with Bristol Colts. He started regularly for the Under 21 team and was soon training with the seniors.

He then went to Cardiff University to read chemistry but after a single term was offered a professional full-time contract and decided to leave university and join the Bristol squad. It was 2002 and he made his debut from the bench against the Wasps at the Queens Park Rangers ground and then gained his first start against the Saracens at Watford. In all, he made seventeen premiership and cup appearances. Unfortunately Bristol were then relegated and found themselves in financial difficulties with a host of highly-paid overseas professionals sitting on their books.

He had been called up for the England Under 21 team and gained two caps against Wales and Italy. He was also selected to go to South Africa but had the intense frustration of having to withdraw due to a hamstring injury.

He then had two seasons in the Championship with Bristol. The first match of these was against the newly-promoted Pirates at the Memorial Ground and Chris played in every match that year culminated by winning the Powergen Shield at Twickenham. The second saw Bristol regaining their Premiership position but Chris had by then found himself frequently on the replacements' bench although he did play in their unexpected home defeat by the Pirates.

The following autumn he joined Jim McKay's Pirates squad on loan for a six week cover for injuries beginning at Bedford and then scoring twice on his home debut against Nottingham at Kenwyn. In all he made just five appearances but enjoyed the experience in Cornwall. Back at Bristol the Shoguns had signed Dan Ward-Smith as a flanker and opportunities were thus likely to be limited.

He took up the chance to join Newbury on the basis that he could still live in Bristol and had been offered a two-year contract. Newbury were on an upward curve at the time, backed by Vodafone, and fielded some useful players including three other future Pirates who were Chris Cracknell, Mark Ireland and Duncan Bell. However, things went badly off the field at Newbury, Vodafone pulled out and Chris clearly needed a club with a brighter future.

He already knew some of the Pirates from his brief sojourn at Kenwyn and after a coffee with Mark Hewitt at Cribbs Causeway just off the M5 he decided to head off once more for Cornwall.

He began well by scoring in both pre-season friendlies and then against his former club when the league season opened against Newbury. His back-row colleagues were Iva Motusaga, Sam Betty, Matt Evans and the Frenchman Bertrand Bedes and soon to be joined by Blair Cowan. In truth it was not a vintage season but Chris cemented his place with some excellent performances and took part in no less than thirty-three of the total of thirty-six matches.

The next three seasons proved to be an outstanding period for the club with the Pirates contesting the Championship playoffs each time and reaching the actual finals on the second and third occasions. Before that, they marched through to the final of the inaugural B & I Cup where they turned over a strong Munster A team to win the trophy itself. On a thrilling night in front of a big noisy crowd at Camborne the back-row of Dave Ward, Blair Cowan and Chris himself played havoc with their Irish visitors. Most fans lining the banks agreed that Chris had rarely performed better and was in the eyes of many the outstanding forward on the field on that glorious sunny May evening.

The following season the Pirates reached the two-legged final with Worcester Warriors having already shared the spoils in two breathlessly close encounters in the regular season. Chris starred in both – again performing magnificently in his understated way – tackling everything that moved, clearing out at the breakdowns and tidying up the loose ball on the ground as though his life depended on it.

In the playoffs he had put in a stellar shift in a big win at Bedford, another in the semi-final with London Welsh and yet again in the finals themselves. All these were on Sky television and their various sages and pundits were all suitably impressed.

The summer break of 2011 involved him having an operation and hence his season was delayed. He was back in time to lead the team to another close win over Munster at Clonmel and the Pirates, and Chris himself, looked poised for a real tilt at the Championship title. His old club Bristol were the promotion favourites but were given a thorough pasting at the Mennaye and all seemed set fair for the final push.

Returning to the Memorial Ground he maddeningly broke his arm during the first half but somehow played in that condition for rest of the match. He was obviously out for the finals and this may have had something to do with such a disappointing outcome against a rather modest and increasingly litigious London Welsh.

He made his comeback again at Bristol late the following September but, after a few games, disaster struck once again and he broke his arm for a second time against Carmarthen Quins. He was out for the rest of the season and was thus condemned to fret from the sidelines. Head Coach Ian Davies shuffled his back-row repeatedly but somehow never quite managed to adequately replace him.

He was back in harness for the new season and was soon performing as well as ever. By this time he was leading the team regularly as Gavin Cattle's appearances became more spasmodic and Chris worked hard to integrate some of the younger recruits into the rigours of Championship rugby. In this he was sufficiently successful for it to be a seamless transition when he became the official club captain in 2014–15 as the Welsh scrum-half concentrated upon his new coaching responsibilities. He finished the season with selection for the Barbarians to play against Heriots in Edinburgh.

Chris is now very much a man of Cornwall having married and settled in Truro where he has started a young family. He hopes to have another couple of years in professional rugby but will aim to move into coaching in due course.

# Iva Motugasa

Position: Flanker
Height/Weight: 6' 0", 15st 2lbs
Date of Birth: 1978
Matches: 111 + 22
Tries: 37

**Did you know?** Iva's nickname 'The Jet' did not refer to his speed around the rugby field but dated back to his martial arts days when he was named after the movie star Jet Li.

Faleiva 'Iva' Motusaga was born in Porirua which is a small city on the north-western shore of Wellington Harbour, New Zealand. His Samoan father had been a boxer and as a child Iva's sports were volleyball and martial arts. Perhaps unusually for a boy growing up in New Zealand he did not take up rugby until he was fifteen years old. He claims that when finally he did so his handling was initially so bad his sports teacher stuck him out on the wing, then tried him at centre and only as a last resort did he put him into the back-row because nobody else wanted to play there.

However it was brought about, it seemed to work well as he was soon playing representative age rugby for Wellington and then later for the Wellington Lions and the Hurricanes. While still at school he joined an old established Wellington club called Poneke initially playing in their Under 21 team.

He made rapid strides at Poneke and in 2000 made his debut for Manu Samoa by coming off the bench against Tonga at Nuku A'lofa and against the Italians at Apia. Hs rugby travels were to also to take him to Europe, Japan and the USA.

In 2004 he decided that he would like to return to Europe to play rugby and see a bit more of the world. By pure fate Iva was ordering a latte and muffin at his local coffee shop when he bumped into an old rugby coach who was then working as an agent for Murray Mexted Sports and soon offered him a contract to play for the Cornish Pirates. One of the attractions was that he already knew the Fatialofa brothers who spoke highly about the club but, by the time he had arrived in Cornwall, they had both signed for Exeter.

He was also to get the opportunity of competing for Samoa in the World Sevens but the combined responsibilities of continued college study and becoming a father for the first time led him to reluctantly pass up the chance. His area of study was in graphic design and before long he was working for an advertising agency in Wellington. Pirates supporters will be well aware of his creative skills in that he designed the new Cornish Pirates logo which has been displayed on shirts, flags, tee shirts and just about everywhere else for the past decade.

He made his debut in the pre-season match with the Cornish All Blacks and his league debut a fortnight later at home to Bristol. Many players take a while to settle into a new environment far away from home but Iva seemed to revel in his new situation from day one. He was an instant hit with supporters due to his wonderfully charming laid-back personality, ready smile and readiness to enjoy both his rugby and his new life in Cornwall. Perhaps it helped that he arrived during a heat wave and that his family were soon able to join him.

In that first season he was a virtual ever-present with twenty-nine appearances during which he notched thirteen tries. The Pirates by then had an outstanding back-row especially when he and Joe Bearman were joined by the big South African Number 8 Lodewyk Hattingh. That season they progressed from being nearly relegation candidates the previous year to a place in the top four prompting owner Dicky Evans to announce the move to Truro and the branding of the Cornish Pirates – complete with Iva's new logo.

The following season at Kenwyn he was again first choice but was twice side-lined by injury and his return was thus reduced to four tries from fifteen starts. He had recovered sufficiently to take on the Harlequins who boasted the famous All Black fly-half Andrew Mehrtens but, having to battle against a dominant pack, could make little impression upon his famous countryman. When the return opportunity came at Truro Iva was again side-lined by injury.

Over the next three seasons Iva was invariably one of the first names on Jim McKay's team sheet and this continued when forwards' coach Mark Hewitt subsequently took over the reins. He had already played a major role in the EDF Trophy victory, appearing in every round, and having an outstanding match in the final at Twickenham.

In 2005 he gained his third full cap for Samoa when lining up against the Wallabies in Sydney. It was a sobering experience in so far as they were trounced to the tune of 74-7 but nevertheless Iva stood out as one of the better players in the Samoan side and received the Man of the Match award from his teammates. He also had the thrill of directly opposing one of his great heroes in George Smith. This however was to prove to be the last of his three caps for the country of his forebears.

At the end of the 2008/09 season both he and Heino Senekal decided to call it a day. He was still playing well and if his blistering pace had lost half a yard he more than made up for it with experience, fitness and a hard competitive edge which contrasted nicely with his sunny disposition off the field.

By the time he decided to retire, he had accumulated nearly forty tries in over a 130 appearances which was an excellent return in a competition as hard-fought as the Championship. His fond memories of Cornwall include being taught to surf by Peter Cook and the support and welcome his family received from the people of Penzance. One incident which stood out for him occurred after his initial home match in a pre-season friendly with Cross Keys when he could be seen running around with a lot of the local kids playing touch rugby – he really felt at home.

While in Cornwall his son Denzel had been joined by a sister Sienna who was born in Truro. The family had planned to return to New Zealand but they stopped off in Sydney to visit his Australian wife's family and decided to set up home there. He had not expected to play rugby but a casual conversation led to him having two years with a great beach club called the Avoca Sharks and he still plays some Golden Oldies rugby once a month.

He has gone back to online graphic design and one of his first jobs in Sydney was working for BLK international sportswear where he had the honour of designing the Manu Samoa 2011 World Cup jersey. Since then he now works for the New South Wales state government but still finds time to do some coaching with the NSW Waratahs Juniors.

Denzel is now fourteen and already playing as a flanker – like father like son.

# Richard 'Rocky' Newton

Position: Wing
Height/Weight: 6'4", 14st 7lbs
Date of Birth: 1979
Matches: 109 + 3
Tries: 119

Did you know? Richard acquired his nickname 'Rocky' when, after a brief fight during his first Redruth Under 16 match, his teammates serenaded the lanky teenager with the 'Rocky' movie theme tune in the dressing room.

Richard Newton was born in Weymouth but moved to Cornwall when his father was transferred to RNAS Culdrose. They moved to Carharrack near Redruth and he began school at Lanner but only took up rugby when he went on to Treliske School. At approximately the same time he began playing mini rugby at Helston.

A close friend was Rob Thirlby who was destined to star with the Saracens, Bath and the England Sevens team and later overlapped briefly with Richard at the Pirates. Accordingly when he moved on to the Richard Lander School he joined Rob and they played together for St Ives at Under 14 level.

During the early 1990s Redruth Colts enjoyed a great reputation for developing talented players and so the two of them moved to the Reds where their respective careers began to flourish. Richard was soon playing for Cornwall Under 18 where his teammates included Joe Bearman from Newquay and Craig Bonds of Redruth. He also had a spell commuting up to Bath to play for their development team and appeared against Leicester and Glasgow.

The coach at Redruth was the ex-Clifton centre Peter Johnson and, just as Richard was doing his A Levels and leaving school, Johnson felt it was time for him to show his considerable paces in the Red's first team. He was very tall and willowy with a devastating burst of speed in his long legs plus a disconcerting hand-off and tries had never been hard to come by.

The season 1997/98 was a pivotal one for Richard. Although Johnson had joined the Pirates, he and Thirlby were by then paid players at Redruth and had the formidable talent of Fijian Nat Saumi setting up the two fliers outside him. However, both he and Nat had been promised a car as part of their deal and when this and other matters were not forthcoming he effectively went on strike.

This was eventually resolved but the thread of trust had been broken and both Richard and Saumi were bound for Penzance. By then he had graduated into the Cornwall team and scored in a heavy win over Hampshire at Redruth followed by a semi-final victory over Gloucestershire when again Richard got a try. This set up the great thrill of facing Cheshire at Twickenham and 30,000 Cornishmen descended once again on the refurbished stadium to cheer on their heroes. There was to be no repeat of 1991 but Richard was on his way.

He had also starred for the Reds in a Cornwall Cup victory over his prospective employers in Penzance in front of the biggest crowd the Mennaye had experienced for years. But once he was installed as one of the Pirates' full-time professionals he could really let rip. The team were still down in South West One and many of the teams they faced were ill-equipped to deal with a back line which boasted not only Richard but Saumi, Victor Olonga, Paul Gadsdon and Steve Evans – all fed by the experienced Mark Roderick. The tries flowed in torrents and Richard filled his boots.

In that first season he ran in thirty tries in all matches and, upon promotion to National III South, scored a mind-blowing forty-three which included thirty-eight in the League alone making him the highest try scorer in England. He had missed the Cornwall Cup final with Launceston in his first season but was back to claim his customary try in the repeat a year later. While the standard of opposition was not always the best, try-scoring at that intensity – including seven in a single match against the Metropolitan Police – could hardly be ignored and he was predictably signed by Cardiff Blues.

His time in Wales proved a disappointment. Although he was working alongside men of the calibre of Rob Howley and Martyn Williams with impressive training and coaching facilities, Cardiff had International wingers available but no regular Second XV at the time. He soon became frustrated and was back at the Mennaye by September 2001.

He had turned out a few more times for Cornwall but had missed the winning Final back at Twickenham due to having just returned from injury. He was back on the wing for another county semi-final at Otley and also against a full Harlequins team who had travelled down to Launceston.

The Pirates were still in National III South but now fought their way up to National II through edging Launceston into second place by a single point at the season's end. However things were all about to change for Richard.

He had put off the chance of going to a university to give professional rugby his best shot but he now decided to join the Royal Air Force and joined the Officer Training College at Cranwell. He returned to play towards the end of the season and to contribute to the final run in for promotion to the Championship but his rugby was by then taking a back seat to his RAF career.

Compared with the army and the Royal Navy, the hierarchy in the air force did not seem to take rugby as seriously and, although he turned out for various RAF teams, he became a little disillusioned. Posted back to St Mawgan, he made a final few appearances for the Pirates in January 2004 and grabbed a try in a vital win in foul conditions at Coventry. A few weeks later the Pirates were thrashed at Orrell and 'Rocky' had played his last game for the Pirates. He was still only twenty-four.

Today he is every inch the confident professional squadron leader who has served in Cyprus, Afghanistan and the Falklands and enjoys his work and family but his rugby days are long behind him. He still follows the game at a distance and visits Cornwall regularly but says he has not been called 'Rocky' for years.

Somewhere along the way he just seemed to fall out of love with rugby but still looks fit enough to pull on a pair of boots tomorrow. Perhaps his career in the sport was only a short one – but nobody accumulated tries quite like Rocky Newton.

# Victor Olonga

Position: Utility Back
Height/Weight: 5'7", 12st 0lbs
Date of Birth: 1974
Matches: 147 + 6
Tries: 142

**Did you know?** Victor's younger brother Henry Olonga was a fast bowler and his country's cricket captain. A politically committed person, Henry ran into deep trouble with Robert Mugabe and once had to flee the country.

Whatever else could be said about him, Victor Olonga was certainly not your typical rugby player.

He was born at Lusaka in Zambia with a Kenyan father and a Zambian mother and two years later he was joined by his younger brother Henry. The family moved to Bulawayo in the Matabeleland region of Zimbabwe where their father ran a medical practice and as a result they both enjoyed a comfortable middle-class upbringing and attended the prestigious Plumtree High School.

Both boys soon showed that they were exceptionally fast runners and their sports-loving father harboured ambitions of them one day representing their country in the Olympic Games. However, it was rugby which gave Victor his best opportunity of expressing himself and he was soon the star centre of both his school and the Bulawayo district. It was at this point that he suffered an incident and a burning sense of injustice which was to have a profound influence upon him.

Victor ideally wanted to play fly-half where he could direct operations but, failing that, to play as an attacking centre. He knew instinctively that he was a far better player than any of the others available but three white boys were selected in midfield and he was stuck out on the wing. Understandably this was something he could neither forgive nor forget.

On leaving school he joined the Bulawayo club Western Panthers and was soon recognised as being one of the outstanding rugby talents that the country had ever produced. He frequently played at full-back where he had the room and the space to maximise the impact of his blistering pace on the hard and often dusty pitches prevalent in the country.

He was soon selected for his country and, although it was back on the wing, he announced his arrival in the most spectacular way possible. The 'Sables' (Zimbabwe's popular name) were at home to Wales in his home city of Bulawayo and, although Wales won, Victor streaked away from his own 22 to score a brilliant solo try leaving the Welsh backs trailing in his slipstream. Just to show that this was no fluke he repeated it with an almost identical effort against the Welsh a week later in Harare.

Over the next five years he appeared regularly for his country both in the full fifteen-a-side game and in international sevens competitions including major tournaments in Dubai and Italy. He played against Wales for a third time – this time at full-back – when he was accompanied by a future Pirates prop named Graham Stewart.

However trouble loomed and, having once refused to play a match in South Africa on account of further patronising treatment from his country's rugby management, he incurred their wrath when the entire team refused to play a match on a diabolical pitch in Mozambique. Victor as the captain was singled out to be the ringleader and was banned by the local Rugby Union.

Fortunately, Dicky Evans had watched him tearing apart all and sundry in a sevens competition and immediately recognised a counter-attacking full-back with the pace of a Christian Cullen but who was now in deep trouble and unable to play. After a couple of discussions had been arranged through intermediaries the brilliant if prickly young man was on his way to Cornwall.

He arrived into a totally different way of life but quickly teamed up with a kindred spirit in the Pirates' other new signing Nat Saumi. The two of them were to spend the next five years together during which time they produced a dazzling array of rugby skills while racking up hundreds of points each season in the process. It was a great relief for Victor to play in an environment where he felt he was properly appreciated and where he could also don the number ten shirt as he had always wished.

He did so for the first time in his third match against Stroud and celebrated by scoring two fine tries. In all he got thirty-three tries during that first season including five in the return match back at Stroud. How they must have dreaded the sight of him.

It must be recognised that he was playing in a relatively low level league and had the luxury of having not only Saumi but the speed of Rocky Newton, the power and steadiness of Steve Evans and the guile of Paul Gadsdon around him. To this could be added a fine experienced scrum-half in Pontypool's Mark Roderick to keep them all supplied with the ball.

Victor was all feints, dodges and tricks and had that murderous burst of speed whenever he found himself in difficulties. He was not always the easiest player to follow as he seemed to play 'off-the-cuff' much of the time and set-plays and overlaps were frequently ignored. The entertainment was brilliant and the Pirates fans loved it – and even opposing supporters had to concede grudgingly that they were watching somebody rather special.

Promotion from South West I was gained that year but Victor's try count (30, 23 and 25) continued over the next three seasons as the Pirates struggled to get up from National III South. Coach Kevin Moseley kept his backs team largely intact although he added two more talented Cornishmen called Andy Birkett and James Hawken to the squad. Victor showed his adaptability and played wherever most needed – fly-half, centre, full-back or even back on the wing. His defence was far better than many gave him credit for and, although a smallish man, could tackle as hard as any. While Saumi was the club's leading goal-kicker Victor also often weighed in with an impressive haul of successful shots at the posts.

Even when playing against amateurs, Victor's ability and speed could not be overlooked and the Harlequins took an interest Once again he was to show an independence of spirit not normally associated with a professional rugby player. He felt that Evans and the Pirates had shown faith in him when he was in the midst of a legal battle over his suspension in Zimbabwe, was enjoying his rugby and was consequently happy to stay loyally where he was and doing what he loved best

Indeed money probably meant rather less to Victor than most and he reportedly sent some of his earnings back to help out rugby in Matabeleland and the Panthers. He was clearly highly intelligent, articulate and widely-read but most of all he was his own man. No honey-tongued agent was ever going to tell Victor Olonga what he should do next.

In 2003 he took part in a third promotion from National II although by now he was appearing frequently on the wing with the more pragmatic Steve Evans at fly-half. A further twenty-five tries were chalked by Victor up as the Pirates sailed serenely up into National I.

Season 2003/04 in League One was a much tougher prospect and turned out to be Victor's Pirate swansong. He opened by scoring another trademark breakaway try in the first match at Bristol and appeared in the big games against Worcester and the Saracens with his last also being against Bristol in the Powergen Shield.

The following year he played for Mounts Bay who were themselves ripping holes in teams in the lower leagues but then returned to Zimbabwe and the Panthers.

Even today he continues to be a newsworthy character in his home country but now has a daughter and runs a market garden back in Matabeleland with an old friend and international rugby colleague Zivanai Dzinomurumbi doing likewise on the next farm.

# Roger Pascoe

Position: Fly Half/Full Back
Height/Weight: 5' 5", 10st 0lb
Date of Birth: 1943
Matches: 1,005 (*c.* 900 first team)
Tries: 52

**Did you know?** Roger's thousand matches for the Pirates may possibly not be unique but there is no record of any player at senior level ever making as many for one club.

To Pirates followers in the 1960s and 1970s little 'Paco' was pure gold. He was a tiny pocket Hercules with hands like flypapers, the sidestep of a matador and could kick a rugby ball with uncanny accuracy.

What Mother Nature had denied him in terms of size and brute strength he compensated for many times over with an outstanding rugby brain. Whether at fly-half or full-back he would catch anything thrown or kicked in his direction with consummate ease and either set up an immediate counter-attack or clear his lines seemingly without pause or indeed much undue effort.

Despite a somewhat baby face, he was a tough little guy on the field with a sharp tongue to match. As a result, big bruising centres and flankers would try to hunt him down but he delighted in jinking effortlessly past them and often made them look foolish in the process. It was this innate sense of self-preservation combined with remarkable consistency which enabled him to clock up a mind-blowing 1005 games for the club's various senior teams over nearly a quarter of a century and he sometimes went an entire season without missing a single match.

Roger was born and bred in Penzance during the Second World War. He was an only child and his father had played football for Penzance so Roger's first interest was in that game. This was to change when he started school at St Pauls Primary where he learned the rudiments of rugby from Pirate full-back Rodda Williams and then under Jimmy Jenkin at Lescudjack. He joined Mounts Bay Colts in 1959 apparently because they had a proper clubhouse where he could hang out with his mates. It immediately became clear that this little chap who then looked about twelve years old had a very special talent.

In September 1961 he was drafted into the team to face an invitation team called the Etceteras. The Pirates were at the height of their powers at the time but fly-half Johnny Thomas was unavailable for the first few matches so the seventeen-year-old was risked in what would probably be a reasonably gentle introduction to first team rugby. A few days later he kept his place to face a London Scottish team bristling with current Scotland internationals. With the experience and protection of Peter Michell at scrum-half, he not only survived but revelled in it. One match later Thomas returned and it was not until the following season that Roger made his breakthrough.

One early experience was against the full Oxford University team who included a particularly violent flanker who hit him repeatedly with a succession of high and late tackles which today would have a referee brandishing a red card in his face. Though obviously bruised and shaken, young Roger did not bat an eyelid and helped steer the Pirates to a highly satisfying 6-0 win. That match was really the making of his career and for the next two decades he was an automatic choice for the team.

The Pirates had a strong fixture list in those days which incorporated Cardiff, Wasps, Saracens, Exeter, Bath and Gloucester and as a result he came up against most of the top fly-halves of the time including the great Richard Sharp on several occasions and rarely suffered by comparison. One of his early games which brought him to more general recognition was a brilliant display against a much-fancied Plymouth Albion team in March 1963.

The great mystery was that, despite all this, the honours in the game always seemed to pass him by. The aforementioned Sharp was the Cornwall and England fly-half and captain and could hardly be deposed but, even after his retirement, the county selectors never seemed to be convinced that the little genius was cut out for the rigours of the County Championship and usually preferred the steady hand of Truro and Gloucester's Tommy Palmer instead.

At full-back Cornwall also had outstanding talents available in Roger Hosen and Graham Bate and thus Roger only managed to play six times for his county when many with only a fraction of his talent got picked year after year. The County Championship in the 1960s and 1970s was the only way Cornish lads could be noticed by the establishment unless they went off to play elsewhere but Roger much preferred to stay with his beloved Pirates.

He made his debut for Cornwall against the British Police in 1963 but only made those paltry six appearances in the county team – all in the fly-half position. His single Championship game was in a fixture postponed due to a foot-and-mouth epidemic against Gloucestershire at Redruth in January 1968.

Back at the Mennaye, year in and year out, Roger continued to produce the goods and his club appearances kept mounting up. By the time of his final season in 1986 a special match against a President's team was arranged to mark his 1,000th match for the Pirates. Furthermore by this time he had amassed over 2,500 points for the club despite not generally being considered as either a front-line goal-kicker or indeed a prolific try-scorer. He was helped by the fact that, despite his small stature, he was sturdily built and never suffered any significant injury apart from once sustaining a broken finger.

He played a full part in the Pirates winning the CRFU Sevens at Camborne in 1964 and appeared in both Cornwall Cup Finals in 1975 and 1976 steering the team home with his accurate kicking and nursing his forwards when they overcame their odds-on opponents from Redruth. He was a popular club captain in 1966/67 and for a second time in 1971/72 and fulfilled the role on dozens of occasions whenever the current captain was unavailable for some reason.

Once he had retired from rugby he was always to be seen following the team and enjoying the company of his old teammates in the bar afterwards. He had threatened to take up bowls at Newlyn but never really got started. Had he ever done so with his competitive instinct he would no doubt have been virtually unbeatable.

Away from rugby Roger followed his father in becoming a motor mechanic variously at Praa Sands, Roseudgeon, Taylors (the garage owned by the former Pirate scrum-half Tinker Taylor beside the bathing pool) and finally for another ex-Pirate Roger Harding at Tolcarne. He was a keen cricketer and, as a batsman and change bowler, played for many years for both Madron and Paul cricket clubs and his son Nick also played his way up through the Pirate ranks.

In January 2002 the whole town was deeply shocked by the sad news that he had collapsed and died suddenly at work in Tolcarne at the age of only fifty-eight.

# Graham Paul

Position: Fly Half
Height/Weight: 5' 7", 10st 7lbs
Date of Birth: 1934
Matches: 104
Tries: 32

**Did you know?** Graham was recruited to play for Bedford after marking out a cross-country course across a farm which just happened to be owned by Bedford's captain.

Graham Paul was born in Penzance and after early school at Lescudjack Primary moved to Penzance Grammar School in 1945 where he quickly established himself as a gifted all-round athlete, excelling at football, the 220 yards and triple jump. His younger brother Trevor followed down the same path but, though a good player in his own right, never matched his elder sibling's achievements.

At that time the school did not play rugby but it did not take long for the lightning-fast little nugget to establish himself in the Pirates Under 15 Colts team as a lively scrum-half.

Signing up for service in the Royal Air Force at seventeen, Graham spent a number of years as Physical Training Instructor being stationed in various parts of the country. He had a few games for Bedford but was soon transferred to Lincolnshire where he ran across a senior officer with connections to the Nottingham Club and thus he turned out for a season at Ireland Avenue and meantime got a taste of county rugby with Notts-Lincs-Derby.

Well aware of the locally-born PTI's rugby prowess, the Pirates' ace committee man and wheeler-dealer Rex Carr pulled a few strings in high places and Graham was conveniently posted back to Cornwall at RAF St Mawgan. Once there, he continued to appear not only for Coastal Command and the RAF itself but by now regularly for the Pirates. In the RAF he rubbed shoulders with rugby league players for the first time and played several times alongside the great Alex Murphy who whetted Graham's curiosity for the professional game although it was to be a few more years before anything happened in this regard.

Although his rugby union career is largely based upon being a very fast fly-half, it was again at scrum-half where he had made his Pirates debut back in December 1951 against the Royal Naval Engineers from Manadon and impressed in a 26-3 victory. Apart from one isolated match in the centre against Redruth, his RAF postings had severely restricted his availability over the next four years although, by now at fly-half, he once tore Truro to shreds on a Boxing Day while home on Christmas leave.

Things changed however in the summer of 1955 when he got that posting back to Cornwall. He was paired up immediately with the ever-reliable and highly resourceful Peter Michell who had also just returned from National Service. The two quickly established themselves as exciting a pair of half-backs as any in the West Country.

Over the next few years their parallel careers continued on an upward curve. Michell was already Cornwall's regular scrum-half but for a couple of years the selectors tended to favour the twinkle-toed talents of another Pirate – Johnny Thomas – to the more explosive running of Graham.

All this changed suddenly in the autumn of 1957 when, having lost their two opening friendlies, the worried Cornwall selectors turned to Graham for the visit of Gloucestershire to Camborne. The transformation was electric as he and Michell steered the Duchy home to a resounding victory. The Cornishmen went from strength to strength and, having seen off the reigning Champions Devon in a group playoff and Hertfordshire at Watford, they faced the might of Lancashire at a Redruth ground packed to the rafters with 20,000 fanatical Cornish fans.

Graham had played a major role in the journey so far but now he faced the toughest test in his career to date. His opposite number was the brilliant Bev Risman whom he would later often face in rugby league and the Lancashire back-row was led by the current England star Alan Ashcroft. Once again Graham rose to the challenge making the vital break for Cornwall's opening try by Mills as Cornwall swept to a thrilling victory.

The 1958 final was played out in vile weather against a Coventry-dominated Warwickshire team packed with current and future England stars. Back in Cornwall his wife Helena was due to give birth to their first child. Having worn themselves to a virtual standstill playing into the driving wind and snow, the Cornwall pack were finally outlasted and it was thirty-three more long years before the Championship would finally be won.

The following season, Graham's form was still so impressive that, when Cornwall came to pick their team, the emerging genius of Richard Sharp had to be found a place in the centre in order to maximise Graham's flair and game management. All appeared set fair and a first England Trial was surely a mere formality when suddenly a huge bombshell was dropped. Graham had joined the Rugby League.

It is hard to understand today quite what this meant for any young man leaving the amateur game to join the professional code. Graham was a talented young man but had just left the RAF and needed a job. He was now married and had started a family. While he was personally very popular and most sympathised and wished him well, the unbending diktats of the Rugby Union were crystal clear – Graham was banned from rugby union for life, could neither play nor coach the sport and was even forbidden to enter the clubhouse or ground. This fate befell anyone who was deemed to have dared to cross to the 'other side'.

Graham's chosen club was Hull Kingston Rovers in East Yorkshire and, while it must have seemed a long way from Penzance, he quickly adapted to the new code and soon became a big local favourite. He made his debut that Boxing Day against York and so began a run of over 200 appearances for the 'Robins'. Before long he was switched to the wing where his blistering pace and bewildering sidestep soon brought him a hatful of tries – thirty-six in a single season – prompting the veteran TV commentator Eddie Waring to dub him with the nickname the 'Cornish Express'.

In all he had six seasons as a professional and finally picked up some of the honours which had eluded him in the union game. He played for a Great Britain team against France at Carcassonne in 1963, featured in a combined Hull team which lost 10-23 to the Australian tourists and this was followed by an appearance at the Wembley Cup Final in 1964 before 85,000 spectators where they went down by 5-13 to Widnes.

On one occasion the two Hull rugby league clubs came down to Penzance to showcase their own code. With regard to those rigid RFU rules, the Pirates could afford him and the enterprise no assistance whatsoever but, as the Mennaye Field was owned by the town council, the rugby league boys could not be prevented from using it. They were however debarred from the clubhouse and Graham even had to rush around and negotiate with a local timber yard to find some replacement goalposts as even these had been cynically removed by some rugby-union-minded zealot.

While he was based in Hull, he had managed both a pub and a hotel and had developed a liking for the trade. In 1965 he brought his family back to Cornwall to become landlord of the aptly-named Sportsman's Arms at Heamoor although for many years he was still debarred from any active role in the sport he loved.

Thankfully this shameful form of sporting 'apartheid' was finally removed and for the past twenty years he has performed all sorts of unsung roles for the club including being a volunteer groundsman where his ready smile and gentle but insightful appreciation of the game is very much valued.

Despite his treatment upon his return from Hull, Graham always realised that none of it was personal and bore no grudges against anyone. Indeed he has nothing but praise for the support he had from the club and all his old teammates – none more so than his old half-back partner Peter Michell who always showed himself to be a loyal and steadfast friend.

# Alan Paver

Position: Prop
Height/Weight: 5' 8", 16st 8lbs
Date of Birth: 1977
Matches: 271 + 61
Tries: 4

Did you know? One of Alan's early jobs before he became a professional rugby player was as a grave digger.

Alan Stephen Joseph Paver was described during a television commentary recently as 'Mister Cornish Pirates' and never has such a compliment been more deserved. Indeed he seems to symbolise everything noble about these rugby underdogs in the remote South West battling to overcome one obstacle after another in their quest to compete with the very best in the land.

He was born in Rotherham but, after his parents separated, he and his mother moved firstly to Lincolnshire and then to Morecambe on the Lancashire coast. Life at Heysham High School was not easy. As with many bright young boys, Alan found his outlet in sport rather than academia, excelling in cricket, boxing, and of course rugby. England coach Stuart Lancaster taught briefly at the school but the true guide and mentor to young Alan was a man called Mike Kirby.

It was Kirby who coached him and promoted his cause to the extent that Alan not only made the school and Lancashire Under 15 teams but also the North of England in a side which included Ian Balshaw and Pat Sanderson. Kirby also pointed him towards the Vale of Lune club a few miles inland. He had by then transferred from the back-row to become a prop and had been selected for Lancashire at Under 18 level. They went on a tour to South Africa and his eyes were opened to not only their intense scrummaging at every level but also the social upheaval engulfing the nation at that time.

At this point the game turned professional and, having tried his hand at several jobs, he decided to have a go himself. He had played sixty matches for the Vale of Lune in League

Two North when he and Sanderson had a few games with Sale who were briefly assisted by Graham Dawe as a player and part-time coach.

In the summer of 1999, Dawe invited Alan to join him at Plymouth Albion where he soon established himself in a powerful front-row with Wayne Reed and Dawe himself. Given that he has now become an honorary Cornishman, he had surprisingly never before been south of Birmingham.

He had three good years in an Albion team which gained promotion in his second season and, appearing against the Pirates on four occasions, made some eighty appearances in all. His biggest match was an exciting Tetley Bitter Cup game against the Harlequins. However, towards the end of his third season, he began looking for another club to further his career.

The Pirates had just won promotion to National II and Kevin Moseley was looking to strengthen his squad and had seen Alan enough times to appreciate the young prop's qualities. In August 2002 Alan came on as a replacement in a friendly against Exeter – now a Pirate for the very first time.

That first season he teamed up with Dan Seal and another ex-Albion man James Owen as the club stormed to a second successive promotion with Alan appearing in every match. As a loose-head prop, he was stocky, immensely strong and already the possessor of a great deal of scrummaging know-how as well as a ready fund of sarcastic one-liners to wind up the opposition!

For the next decade Alan was an automatic choice whenever he was fit and available and added to his repertoire by being able to perform on the tight-head side equally well. Indeed a strong man with an exceptional technique who is only five-feet-eight inches with his boots on can pose hideous problems for a taller prop and Alan thrived upon this.

That technique was honed over countless hours of scrummaging practice by a man who has developed an encyclopaedic knowledge of the 'dark arts' – a subject he will wax upon for hours if ever given the chance. In this he has been a role model for a string of young props who have come through the club during his time.

Alan took a full part in the EDF Trophy run and the Final, the B & I Cup and both the Championship playoffs and thus shares with Gavin Cattle the honour of having been an integral part of all those major landmarks. He was never a great try scorer but one he did get in the EDF Trophy on a vile night of driving snow back in his native Yorkshire somehow seems to summarise his entire career in a few breathless seconds.

The score was 17-11 to Leeds but, with injury time ebbing away fast, the Pirates pack smashed its way back into the Leeds 22 and a furious rolling maul took them up to the try-line. There was a heaving bout of mud wrestling during which the Pirates forwards first crabbed sideways and then drove over in a mass of flailing arms and legs. Mr Small, the referee, gave the try and, of all people, it was a grinning Alan who arose last like a mud-encrusted gnome proudly clutching the ball. Di Bernardo converted and the rest is history.

His benign influence on the squad itself and the team's relationship with its supporters and the general public has been huge. On the field he is a tough hard-nosed competitor but, once off it, his face lights up easily into a broad smile that would melt an iceberg. Despite his northern roots he has become a part and parcel of Penzance, where he also resides, and seems to have time for everybody in the town. New players are always made welcome, media men are indulged and fans are always warmly embraced. He even took up salsa dancing when his Cuban neighbour encouraged him to go along.

Now into his late thirties he has continued to turn in high quality performances although recently his appearances have frequently been interrupted by injuries. Nevertheless he has made well over 300 appearances for the Pirates which are a huge total for one club performing at a professional level.

He was recognised by being selected for the Championship team which played the Maoris at Doncaster and, after having had to withdraw from one invitation to represent them due to injury, finally gained the honour in 2014 of becoming a Barbarian at Bath when playing against the Combined Services. Although always remaining loyal to the Pirates, Alan also briefly experienced Premiership rugby when he was loaned to the Exeter Chiefs where he faced one of his rugby idols Carlos Nieto.

For the past year he has taken on the expanded role of Player/Coach with obvious concentration upon the forwards but has still managed to play a significant number of matches and has enjoyed something of a renaissance as one of the most experienced players in the Championship.

All in all 'Paves' is a very special Pirate.

# Harvey Richards

Position: Fly Half
Height/Weight: 5' 10", 10st 0lbs
Date of Birth: 1925
Matches: 252
Tries: 42

**Did you know? Harvey was a pupil at Truro school with Hollywood film star Robert Shaw.**

Henry Harvey Richards was born in Newlyn as the son of a schools attendance inspector. He began school at Tolcarne and started watching Newlyn play rugby at their old St Goulder ground perched high up above the town.

He was clearly a lad with plenty of ambition and initiative as he took himself off to Truro, presented himself to the headmaster of Truro School and calmly asked to sit the entrance exam. Needless to say he passed and his career took off from there both in the personal and the rugby sense. He played regularly for Truro School which was more than could be said for another pupil, John Kendall-Carpenter, who was also a contemporary but showed little early promise on the rugby field. His great days were to come later.

When it became time for him to leave school the entire country was locked in the throes of the Second World War. Turning eighteen, Harvey joined the Royal Navy Volunteers at Devonport and, serving in motor launches, saw action in Germany. As someone who already showed leadership skills and immediately attracted respect, he was commissioned as a Sub-Lieutenant by the time the war ended. When he turned out in the first ever match for the newly-formed Penzance and Newlyn against Guy's Hospital in September 1945 he was actually home on leave from his base in Scotland.

He had already played an active role in helping to prepare the old rubbish dump-cum-parade ground to become the Mennaye and to be ready in time to open its gates as a rugby field. Thus the very roots of the club are embodied in Harvey and his friends and colleagues of the time.

On demobilisation his life was spent in education working as a schoolmaster and later a headmaster. Before that he naturally had to qualify and so attended Westminster College in

London to study English and Physical Education. Although he could perform equally well as a scrum-half it was at fly-half that he now began to make his mark. Living and studying in London, he joined Rosslyn Park and for the next few seasons turned out regularly for them as well as playing for the Public School Wanderers both of which were regular visitors to Penzance each September. Rosslyn Park had some brilliant backs at the time including the future England men Chris Winn and Brian Boobbyer and it was Harvey's job to make it all happen for them.

In all he made over fifty first team appearances for Park and enjoyed playing against the Harlequins at Twickenham and also at places like Leicester, Cardiff and Newport against all the top performers of that era. He was also capped six times for Middlesex despite being a proud Cornishman.

His time in London obviously meant that his appearances for the Pirates were severely limited until he returned home in 1949 to take up a teaching post at St Ives Junior School where he was to work for the rest of his rugby-playing career. He linked up with scrum-half and captain Tinker Taylor and they formed a formidable partnership. The previous season they had enjoyed several County Championship games together for Cornwall but now, back on the Mennaye Field with the raw power of Ginger Williams and Mike Terry outside them, they could really take command.

The following year Taylor had begun to devote more time to his garage business and family and Harvey was joined by the younger Peter Michell with a quick pass and a left foot to die for. Harvey played his part in developing the blossoming talents of the young scrum-half and by the time the historic season of 1952–53 arrived they had already notched up fifty First XV matches together.

Harvey was elected captain for that season and what a year that was! It is easy to forget these days just how much rested upon the shoulders of the 'skipper' in those days before coaches, team managers, analysts and the like. They led the training, organised the practice sessions, helped select the team, decided on the tactics, bought the beer, led the singing and above all set the tone of the team and the men within it.

By this time Harvey was, despite his light frame (even for the time when rugby players were far less bulky than they are today), an experienced campaigner, a shrewd tactician but above all a leader who believed in togetherness, team spirit and enjoying rugby for its own sake. As the weeks and months rolled by and the team went from victory to victory, this loyal band of brothers welded themselves ever closer together.

By the New Year the Pirates remained undefeated and continued to be so for many more weeks to come. There were some desperately close calls as other clubs tried frantically to unseat them but, under Harvey's guidance, they somehow pulled themselves through to a breathless draw or yet another narrow victory. By the time their colours were finally lowered by an ecstatic Redruth team on the Mennaye it was already March.

He had only one more full season but by then his work and family began to dominate his time. In due course he took over as the Deputy Head of the Alverton School and then became the Headmaster of Heamoor County Primary – a job he loved and remained there for twenty years until he finally retired.

One of his fondest memories was when Bill McLean's Wallabies made their tour base at the Queens Hotel in Penzance at the end of the long hot summer of 1947. Among their pre-tour baggage they had been loaned a real live Wallaby from London zoo and the team were charged with looking after it – a task they apparently shared with some of their hospitable Pirate friends. Needless to say one evening it 'escaped' and Harvey recalls hordes of rugby players, policemen, children, old ladies, servicemen on leave and assorted townspeople chasing this poor animal around Penlee Gardens. Benny Hill would have loved it!

Away from rugby – but never that far away – Harvey also loved music and to lead the singing in his rich baritone voice with the old Cornish songs and hymns as his particular favourites. There were many nights in the Pirates' bar at the back of the Union Hotel in the days before the club took over Westholme when the lads raised the roof – usually led by Harvey. Rugby teams and deep lifelong friendships are forged unbreakably that way.

Off the field his rugby activities were far from done. For nine years he was a Cornwall selector at a time when county rugby occupied a much greater position in the public consciousness than it does today. He was also the leading light in the establishment of mini-rugby in primary schools in Cornwall and in time spreading it to the clubs thereby attracting youngsters from countless non-rugby-playing schools as well. Many young and now not-so-young local rugby men owe their start in the game to his energy and vision.

As a life-long friend and indeed best man at the wedding of John Kendall-Carpenter, he was a moving spirit in the trust set up to honour the great man's memory and to provide sporting facilities and opportunities for young people in Cornwall.

In the mid-1990s he served as President of the CRFU and also founded the 'Sages' which is a monthly lunch club for old Cornish rugby players who get together over a beer and a pasty to relive their glory days and perhaps to bemoan the shortcomings of modern rugby.

With Harvey in the chair a rousing chorus or two is surely never far away as true rugby men forget their old aches and pains for an hour or so with a laugh and a sing-song and to remember just how much fun rugby football can be.

# Duncan Roke

Position: Centre/Full Back
Height/Weight: 6' 2", 14st 9lb
Date of Birth: 1974
Matches: 47 + 4
Tries: 10

Did you know? The 6-feet 2-inch-tall Duncan was a mere 5 foot 4 inches tall when he left school to begin college.

Duncan Roke was born in Malta where his father was then serving in the Royal Marines. The family returned to the UK and settled in Tavistock from where Duncan attended Plymouth College as did two other future Pirates Will James and Andy Birkett. His brother was also a good player who featured for Tavistock RFC and also, while serving in the RAF, for Glamorgan Wanderers.

Duncan enjoyed rugby but did not excel at it for the simple reason he was a late developer and hence very small as a teenager who actually gave up the game completely for two years. He went to Cardiff University but came home after a year and worked at a factory in Tavistock at which point he shot up in height, took up rugby again and turned out for the local team.

In 1994 he took himself off to Nottingham Trent University where he studied Sports Sciences and first began to play serious rugby mainly as a fly-half. It was there that he came to the notice of the Leicester Tigers who invited him to join their Development Squad while continuing with his studies at Nottingham.

His time at Leicester gave him access to some high-quality coaching and fitness work but opportunities at first team level were always likely to be few and far between. The Tigers could call upon stars like Pat Howard and Will Greenwood as their centres and had England's Tim Stimpson plus the budding genius of Geordan Murphy covering the full-back berth. In four seasons at Welford Road he featured in only six senior matches but in a large number for the A team.

It was time to move on and at twenty-four he had attracted interest from Leeds and Worcester but decided to go to Henley instead. It must be remembered that at the time the Hawks were a highly efficient organisation and had numbered Clive Woodward among their recent coaches. The rugby facilities were excellent and job opportunities in the locality to combine with playing rugby were plentiful. He joined the pharmaceutical industry working in the monitoring of clinical trials and this was a job which gave him sufficient time to train and play as a part-time professional.

While at the Hawks he worked with Jim McKay who was instrumental in using Duncan as a full-back. During his time at Henley they gained promotion from National Two and he amassed over sixty league matches along the way.

In 2000 he was selected for an English National Divisions representative team which played the South Africans at Worcester and shocked the visitors by winning. On the strength of his performance, Duncan was asked to join the Warriors as a fully-fledged professional. They were by now on the cusp of qualifying for the top flight and included Scotland's Ben Hinshelwood in their backs. Promotion did not come immediately but in 2004, at the third time of asking, a move up to the Premiership was finally secured. When they eventually did so, Duncan played a leading role by scoring twice in the vital deciding match with Bristol.

The Warriors team that year included a number of future Pirates including Wes Davies, Matt Evans and Rhodri McAtee all of whom moved down to Cornwall without appearing in the Premiership. Duncan stayed on for another season but by then the famous Springbok Thinus Delport had arrived so consequently his outings were limited to just a few matches in the European Shield. It was frustrating and at thirty-one and, having just become a father for the first time, he was unsure as to whether to continue in professional rugby.

It was at this point that the Cornish Pirates and their move to Truro were launched and, picking up on all the excitement generated, his agent suggested them as an attractive prospect. He met up with his former coach McKay and was suitably impressed with the Australian's passion and vision for the future and so he brought his young family to Penzance.

He made his debut in a pre-season match at Launceston and found himself in a far stronger team than the one which had twice been unceremoniously butchered by Worcester two years earlier. His cool, measured approach and stern defensive qualities helped bring the best out of younger fliers like McAtee, Richard Welding and Matt Jess. Indeed the star-studded Harlequins were the only team to comprehensively defeat the Pirates that season apart from one of those occasional inexplicably dire displays at Rotherham.

The next season proved to be his last in professional rugby and finished with a glorious climax. Earlier in the season he had shown outstanding form against Exeter at Camborne scoring twice and cutting repeatedly through the hard-hitting Fatialofa brothers in the Exeter midfield into the bargain.

The EDF run saw him play a leading role in the thrilling victories over Leeds, Doncaster and Plymouth Albion before stepping out at Twickenham to renew his acquaintance with the Fatialofas and the rest of Exeter Chiefs. His abiding memory of that day was walking around the pitch at the end with the trophy, clutching his little son George in his arms while basking in the sunshine and the acclaim of the adoring Pirates fans. Rugby just doesn't get any better than that and Duncan decided that was how it all should end. It was his last-ever game of serious rugby and so he went out on the crest of a wave.

His rugby career began rather later than most but he had accumulated a fair amount of recognition along the way. He played for the England Sevens Team, the Barbarians on a couple of occasions and for Mickey Steele-Bodger's celebrated team in their traditional autumn match at Cambridge. He had also found time to play some Minor Counties cricket for Devon.

Since leaving Cornwall he has moved back near Worcester to Bromsgrove where he has coached at the local club who ply their trade in National Two North. He has also returned to the healthcare industry working for a large medical devices corporation named Medtronics. He continues to take an interest in the Pirates and can often be seen in the stands whenever they play in the Midlands.

# Nat Saumi

Position: Full Back (Utility Back)
Height/Weight: 5' 11", 14st 7lbs
Date of Birth: 1972
Matches: 123 + 3
Tries: 88

**Did you know?** Nat Saumi was one of the very first Fijians to come to play professional rugby in the United Kingdom and one of the longest to stay.

Fijian international sevens star Nacanieli Saumi was born in Fiji, brought up in the capital Suva and played his club rugby for a club on the outskirts of the city called Nabua. The club has been re-launched a couple of times but traces its origins to a Methodist Youth organisation in the early 1960's. Nat himself, as a committed Christian and family man was, and indeed remains, very much an embodiment of this and has recently returned to Nabua and its activities after a seventeen-year marathon in Cornwall and Plymouth.

Having come to prominence on the sevens circuit in Hong Kong, he came to the UK with a sevens touring side called the Fiji Spartans which included the famous Waisale Serevi and starred in the Henley Sevens.

Nat moved to Redruth for the 1996–97 season and played at the Mennaye Field alongside Richard Newton in a county semi-final when the Reds defeated the Pirates by a 21-6 score line. By this time both he and Newton had decided to leave and follow their former Head Coach Peter Johnson, who had already switched from Redruth to Penzance the previous summer.

It is always dangerous to try to compare players from different eras particularly when the quality of opposition varies so widely. Nevertheless, as the Pirates embarked upon a drive up through the English league system between 1998 and 2003, there can be no question that Nat was any other than a simply outstanding performer wherever and whenever he was asked to play.

As with many talented Fijians, he had the transferable rugby skills to perform anywhere behind the scrum and appeared to do so with consummate ease. In addition he was a veritable points-scoring machine racking up an extraordinary total of just under 2,000 points in a mere 126 matches. This total would have been even higher had his entry into his second season not been delayed until late November.

When he made his debut against Exeter in a pre-season friendly he was joining a back line with exceptional talent, pace and physical strength for the level of opposition they encountered. Besides Newton, Johnson already had the powerful Welshman Steve Evans and the superb Paul Gadsdon on his books. He now added a further element with the Zimbabwean flyer Victor Olonga.

Nat started out at full-back and appeared there in every match that season except one. Ironically this was against the Fijian national team which opened its UK tour at the Mennaye and, having shaken off the worst of their jet-lag, took the plucky Pirates apart in the second half.

However, most games were very much the other way around as the Pirates took the South West One league title at a canter in an avalanche of tries. Nat scored four in a match on two occasions and personally notched up forty-two points in the demolition of Berry Hill. Additional joy came Nat's way with the Pirates winning the Cornwall Cup for the first time since 1976 when they convincingly defeated a fourteen-man Launceston at Redruth with Nat being very much the Man of the Match.

He began the next season late but his first two matches back were by pure coincidence against his former club Redruth. They were both nail-biting games with the first a 22-22 draw and the second a narrow 20-21 defeat. Perhaps that delay had some bearing on the fact that a second immediate promotion was missed by narrowly losing out to Esher despite annihilating the Metropolitan Police by a farcical 136-6 score in the last home game. Some consolation came to Nat from a repeat Cornwall Cup win again over Launceston in a much better game than the previous year.

By now Nat had shown himself to be a wonderfully elusive runner with excellent hands as one might expect from a skilled sevens player. He was also a destructive tackler and an increasingly reliable goal-kicker particularly from short range as his enormous number of conversions would testify.

The Pirates were by now acknowledged professionals playing in leagues where most opponents were still turning out just for match fees and expenses. Occasionally an element of jealousy and spite would be directed against them both from opposing players and the often small but vocal minority of spectators at certain away fixtures. Sadly the players in general – but Nat and Victor in particular – occasionally had to endure some rough handling on the park and outbreaks of unpleasant abuse from the side-lines.

Inexperienced referees could sometimes also be overly influenced by this vitriolic hubbub and Nat once found himself the victim of an unwarranted red card during a match at Gloucester Old Boys. He was subsequently cleared by a RFU Disciplinary panel and was back two weeks later to face the same opponents in a return fixture. Revenge is sweet and he probably gained a certain grim satisfaction in kicking thirteen conversions plus scoring two tries of his own in completely shredding them in another hundred-point debacle.

In 1999 Nat also played for Cornwall in the County Championship in both the semi-final against Cheshire at Redruth and the Twickenham Final against Gloucestershire when the Cornishmen claimed the title for only the third time in their long history. He appeared at Twickenham with three other Pirates – Steve Larkins, Kevin Moseley and Jason Atkinson – but it was the strong running and counterattacks from Nat which tipped the game in the favour of the Cornishmen. Hence he finished that season having won the South West I, Cornwall Cup and County Championship titles.

It took three years for the club to haul themselves out of National Three South but, having done so in 2002 when Nat personally contributed no less than 376 points, they proceeded to run away with the National Two title at the first time of asking with Nat once again at the centre of everything.

The next season 2003/04 saw Nat at last performing in National One where he could measure his skills against opponents who could potentially match his abilities. Unfortunately it was to be at Plymouth Albion rather than with the Pirates. Promotion had been secured among much rejoicing on the Mennaye against Stourbridge but it proved to be Nat's final appearance. Training ground flare ups are not uncommon in any rugby club but one had spilled over badly and Nat's time at Penzance and Newlyn came to a sad and abrupt end.

Going into the new season it became obvious just how much the Pirates were going to miss him. They had entered what is now the Championship without their most potent strike runner and furthermore having lost their prime goal-kicker whom they had disastrously failed to replace. Meanwhile Nat settled in at Plymouth where he immediately showed that he could perform with distinction at that level where he formed a powerful centre partnership with the chunky Tongan Keni Fisilau.

Nat played several times against the Pirates over the next few years either in the centre or at full-back and always seemed to pull out that little bit extra against the club that had let him go. In 2008, and by then in his mid-thirties, he began to assist Graham Dawe in coaching the backs and in early 2012 took over from Peter Drewett who had briefly replaced Dawe as Director of Rugby at the club.

His tenure at the helm was not an easy time for Albion who suffered from a severe lack of funding but he nevertheless kept them safely embedded in the Championship although he never quite managed to get one over on the Pirates during all the time he was in overall charge.

In late 2013 he decided that it was time to take his family back to Fiji where he has worked for the Government in the sports development of youngsters not only in rugby but also in cricket and now commands a high position in the world of sport in Fiji.

Few overseas players have spent such a prolonged period in the UK. Sadly he never quite got the opportunity to play in the Premiership (as he was also involved with his university studies and IRB coaching certificates) or in European competitive rugby despite many with far less talent having often done so.

However, as a points-scoring machine Nat Saumi has had few peers.

# Dan Seal

Position: Prop
Height/Weight: 6' 1", 17st 7lb
Date of Birth: 1979
Matches: 122 + 93
Tries: 4

**Did you know?** When at school Dan was a classmate of Formula 1 driver Jenson Button.

There was no rugby tradition in the family when Dan was born in Frome. His father had played a bit of local football but when his son started school he realised that his young lad needed an outlet for his boundless energy and sent him along to the Under Six minis at Frome RFC.

The quiet Somerset town has never been a major rugby centre but the club had a well-developed structure through the age groups and Dan progressed up through the teams and played for Somerset and South West Clubs at both Under 17 and Under 19 Levels. His secondary school never played rugby so that route was effectively denied to him.

On leaving Oakfield School he began to train as a motor mechanic. One of his coaches had a link with Bath and in 1998 he moved there to play regularly for their youth teams. Here he came under the coaching guidance of ex-Pirate hooker John Kimberley and in particular the former flanker Nick Maslen. He trained on Monday and Wednesday nights and had regular matches at weekends while continuing to work away during the day repairing tiny Renault 2CVs.

Dan had two seasons with the Bath Youth team which included some notable future star players including hooker Lee Mears and the Cornish winger Tom Voyce. Also numbered in the squad was the giant lock-forward Olly Hodge who was later to play a part in bringing Dan to Penzance. He graduated up to the Bath United team but the club already had many fine props including Victor Ubogu, David Barnes and Kevin Yates two of whom were capped by England. Dan learned much from training regularly with them and his entire game improved but his prospects of regular senior rugby did not seem particularly rosy.

By April 2001 he was restless enough to be looking for another club. Pirates' coach Kevine Moseley was on the lookout for some props and locks and in the end brought four of them down from Bath. The most newsworthy was the ex-England lock Martin Haag who had been brought up in St Ives but he was to be joined by Hodge, Stuart Meddick and Dan himself on a loan deal.

Immediately he joined, Dan found himself caught up in the middle of a major row between the Pirates and the Cornwall Rugby Union over a postponed Cup Final against Launceston at Redruth. The CRFU had ruled that Dan and the Pirates' other two new props were ineligible to play as they had not been at the club when the original game had been scheduled. As the club now had insufficient registered props as a direct result of that particular ruling, the rule book obsessives on the organising committee bizarrely disqualified the club from participation.

Dan made his debut in happier circumstances against Blackheath and went on to play twenty-eight times that season. In fact he took part in many more matches as he was still playing for Bath United. He was representing the Pirates on a Saturday and then racing around the country to turn out for Bath United on the Monday night. On one occasion he actually switched team buses at a motorway service station.

That season the Pirates won the National III South League to pip Launceston by winning the final match at Westcombe Park. That League title was followed by another when the Pirates bounced straight up through National II in a single season. Dan had by then been joined by Alan Paver and the two struck up a tremendous partnership playing virtually every match together for the entire season. Having survived two whole years of matches virtually unscathed, Dan finished the season nursing a broken jaw resulting from an unfortunate incident on the training pitch.

Over the six succeeding seasons he appeared in most match day squads but by then had serious rivals for his tight-head prop position initially from Nick Adams and later from Sam Heard. He was seldom flashy (although when he did score a try he loved to celebrate it) but teammates and supporters all respected him for his rock-like solidity, mobility and hard competitive edge.

Dan outlasted his rivals and, by the time he departed in 2009, he had amassed well over 200 competitive matches for the club. He played his part throughout the EDF run in 2007 and thoroughly enjoyed his one appearance at Twickenham for the Final itself when an entire bus load of family and friends came up from Frome to support him. One of his memories of the match was of receiving a bad cut on the head and praying that Jan Rendall could somehow slap enough grease over it to prevent the referee insisting he should have to go off. That season had begun in frustrating fashion when he was injured in the opening game at Camborne and had missed much of the autumn as a result and so he certainly did not want it to end in the same way.

Dan loved Cornwall and actually played for the county team on several occasions between 2004 and 2006 when he usually partnered Sam Heard and Villi Ma'asi.

It was therefore particularly difficult for him when he had to leave. He had just bought a house but had come to the end of his current contract. That summer there was a change in the coaching regime with Brett Davey departing and the new team of Stirling, Davies and Biljon yet to arrive. In the meantime Dan was somehow allowed to slip through the cracks while some palpably less able props remained at the club.

Having spoken to Coventry, he was persuaded by Russell Earnshaw to join the Birmingham-Solihull Bees which initially seemed a good solution. There was one huge snag – the Bees were flat broke and nobody was getting paid. By October it had become intolerable and he was on his way again to Bedford with a part-time contract. This entailed him having to find other work which in his case has involved teaching and coaching at various schools and colleges – mainly rugby but also cricket and hockey.

Bedford proved a good move and he made around a hundred Championship appearances for them before knee injuries began to take their toll. Indeed he must have spent a great deal of time in the treatment room as he ended up by marrying one of the club's physiotherapists.

He will always have a special place in the affections of Pirate fans as he was always reliable, never took a step backwards and was as good a scrummager as any in the Championship. He rated his most difficult opponent as the notoriously grumpy and taciturn Tom Smith of Northampton and Scotland who was a small compact loose-head prop of the Alan Paver variety and as a result was a nightmare to scrummage against.

Dan recently took up a new role as forwards coach at Ampthill RFC where he will link up again with his old friend Vili Ma'asi.

# Heino Senekal

Position: Lock
Height/Weight: 6' 7", 17st 0lbs
Date of Birth: 1975
Matches: 105 + 11
Tries: 9

Did you know? Heino was occasionally teased at the Pirates for having such massive calves that no socks could be found which he was able to pull up properly and so often played with them hanging around his ankles.

Johannes Hendrik Senekal was born in the small mining town of Tsumeb in the northern Oshikoto region of Namibia. His father had also been a leading rugby player who had himself played for the region that was then known as South West Africa. That national team are popularly known locally as the 'Welwitchias' which is actually the name of a large and extremely ugly plant that is indigenous to the region.

Heino grew up watching his father play rugby and started in the game at his local junior school where he showed considerable promise. As a teenager he went to the Orange Free State in South Africa to study at the Sentraal High School in Bloemfontein and while there his rugby really took off.

It was then off to college in Pretoria where he studied Logistics Management. While there he was asked to attend trials for Namibia itself with a view to the forthcoming World Cup to be held in in Europe.

On the back of this he received his first professional opportunity with the Boland Cavaliers in that beautiful wine growing area and it was indeed the wine trade that Heino returned to when he first came home after retiring from rugby.

The Cavaliers, with Springbok Marius Joubert playing in their backs, had a season to remember and finished third overall in the Currie Cup which was no mean feat for a relatively small provincial team.

In 1998 he had made his international debut for Namibia against the Ivory Coast in the somewhat unlikely venue of Casablanca in Morocco. The following year he went to the first of his three World Cups which took place in France. He played well against the Fijians at Beziers and Canada at Toulouse but probably learned more against France itself in Bordeaux where he faced Olivier Brouzet and Fabien Pelous.

In 2002 he had the opportunity to come to the United Kingdom with an offer from Cardiff Blues. The South African coach who had made the connection had already moved on by the time Heino arrived and he now worked under Dai Young. He made his debut against Leinster that September and was a regular that season starting some twenty-five matches and getting a try against neighbours Swansea. He found the cold and wet of South Wales rather hard to cope with after the hot dry atmosphere in South East Africa but enjoyed the rugby itself.

The next season was World Cup time again and he was off to Australia where he took part in all four matches lining up against Argentina on the Gold Coast, Ireland in Sydney (where he got a yellow card), the Wallabies at Adelaide and finally crossed over to Tasmania to play Rumania. He felt that the Namibians were prepared poorly for the tournament and consequently lost each game but the experience was nevertheless valuable.

On his return it took him a while to achieve the level of match fitness he required and thus to get himself re-established. Young had a link with the Pirates' CEO David Jenkins and as a result the newly-appointed coach Jim McKay invited Heino down to Cornwall. In view of his lack of enthusiasm for the British climate his first impressions cannot have been very encouraging. He arrived in Penzance in the middle of a raging storm during which a temporary stand at the Mennaye Field collapsed in the gale.

Whatever McKay said to him seemed to have worked and just a few days later Heino was trotting out to make his Pirates debut at Number 8 against Bedford. He was actually replacing another Southern African in Matt Evans who had received a bad knee injury a few weeks earlier. Very shortly after his arrival he was joined by yet another big South African called Lodewyk Hattingh. As the Pirates already had the enormous Will James in the pack, McKay could certainly not now complain of any lack of ballast when he needed it.

Following Hattingh's arrival, Heino went back to the second-row displacing Martin Morgan to accompany James. Within weeks they were relishing a rare old battle at Exeter with the Baxter brothers and a week later he played a leading role in overturning promotion-bound Bristol on their own patch. Bristol have often been defeated in Cornwall but this was the only occasion the Pirates have won at the Memorial Ground and in doing so Heino's line-out dominance proved decisive.

The next season saw him back in Africa until mid-Autumn when he came off the bench against the Harlequins at The Stoop. The Quins had already been playing havoc with the Pirates' line-out but as soon as Heino was brought on he was immediately going off again with a yellow card. Not his finest hour.

For the next three years he was an almost automatic first choice and was a key man in the EDF Trophy victory at Twickenham as well as in all the breathless cup ties. James moved on to Gloucester but the ex-Wasp Joe Beardshaw had already come in and the two formed a fine partnership until injury curtailed Joe's career. Heino soldiered on being joined by yet another big aggressive South African named Bruce Cumming.

In 2007 he took part in his third World Cup in France receiving his twenty-seventh and final cap against Georgia in Lens. By this time Heino had become something of a cult figure at Camborne. His charging runs up the middle had earned him the affectionate nickname of 'Heino the Rhino', he was hard and strong and possibly as good a line-out jumper as any in the Championship. He had the happy knack of rising to the big occasion and perhaps his most outstanding game in a Pirate shirt was against Northampton at Franklins Gardens. By the end many discerning Saints supporters were wondering just who this big man careering about the pitch might be.

Like many others his highlight was the EDF win at Twickenham and he actually enjoyed playing in the burning heat that afternoon. He soon got to love Cornwall, the beaches and the Pirates' supporters whom he described as 'real rugby people'

In his last season he was joined in the second-row by Ben Gulliver from Plymouth Albion and played for the Barbarians against Blackheath – the third Pirate to be so honoured that year.

By April 2009 he was approaching thirty-four. He had met his French wife while she had been working in Cornwall and was by now the father of a small child and his thoughts were clearly turning towards home. It was a sad day when both he and Iva Motusaga decided to retire after the final game of that season against London Welsh.

Since returning to Africa he has worked in marketing for Orange River Wines and then came home to take over his father's retail business. He has done some junior coaching and was reported as recently as May 2014 to have made a one-match comeback for a Namibian Legends team in a fund-raising charity event.

# Brian 'Stack' Stevens

Position: Prop
Height/Weight: 5' 11", 15st 6lbs
Date of Birth: 1940
Matches: 493 (Over 500 club games)
Tries: 41

**Did you know?** During his England days rugby was still rigidly amateur and travel expenses for squad sessions were consequently meagre in the extreme. Stack usually got over this by hitching a lift up to London on a broccoli lorry.

Despite the coming of professionalism over the past twenty years, Claude Brian Stevens remains the most celebrated player to have ever risen directly from the ranks of the Pirates. He was born into in a farming family as the youngest of six children at Godolphin during the Second World War. He went to school nearby at Leedstown with another Pirate Roger Roberts and, although it had no organised rugby, their schoolmaster Max Biddick played for Camborne and impromptu games were held. Brian clearly loved it and joined the Mounts Bay Colts team in 1956.

He was a precocious talent and a tough early developer but was lucky in that Mounts Bay were coached by the ex-Pirate prop Ben Jelbert. Perhaps due to his influence Brian became a prop although in his early career he played almost anywhere in the pack. His first team debut was at Number 8 when he was drafted in for a match against the Coastal Command in November 1958.

It was about this time that he acquired the name 'Stack' which is now how he is universally known around the rugby globe although he is still called Brian by his family and neighbours. The story of its origin is that he was playing cards and, having run a bit short of money, continued to stack rather than place a bet until an exasperated teammate named Tony Stevenson called him 'Stack'.

Another version insists that he acquired the nickname when he gave the excuse that he was busy stacking corn for being late for pre-season scrummaging practice and was promptly told 'Well go and stack that b***** scrum.' Whichever version you prefer 'Stack' certainly stuck!

His big chance came the following February when he replaced Harvey Jose to prop against Redruth at the Mennaye. The Reds were missing some of their formidable Cornwall front row but the prospect for a teenager making only his second first-team appearance was still a daunting one. The Pirates beat the Reds for the first time for three long years and he was on his way.

Big games followed including a victory over the Wasps facing the England prop Gordon Bendon and the glamour fixture against Cardiff. Next he made his first away trip to South Wales. The Pirates took only a small squad and he found himself playing in the front-row in four brutally hard matches – including one against Aberavon and their current Wales prop Les Cunningham – in a mere five days.

That summer Irish prop Tony Byrne joined the club and Stack began the season as a lock against AS Milano. However, it was as a prop that he was picked for his Cornwall debut against a United Hospitals team in a friendly at Camborne. It was a relatively easy introduction to county rugby but this was to change a few days later when Surrey came to Penzance in a thick fog and, despite claiming a try, he was given a torrid evening by Surrey's Polish prop Karl Wronski.

His career at the Pirates continued to blossom and the club were enjoying a golden era when they became perhaps the strongest team in the South West Cornwall made it to the semi-final at Twickenham that season but the selectors had decided to play safe with the aforesaid Tony Byrne. There was consolation in that the Pirates showed their calibre by defeating not only the Saracens but, on an evening of high drama, mighty Cardiff as well.

Then came a setback. During the first game of the following season he broke his ankle and missed the entire autumn, the county games and any outside chance of meeting the Springboks. However by Christmas he was back and by the next year he was back in the Cornwall team. They again made the semi-finals at Coventry where he found himself taking on the fearsome Warwickshire front rank of Judd, Godwin and McLean.

For the next few years he turned in a host of fine performances and received a reserve card for an England trial at Fylde in 1964 but heard no more. Then, as his older colleagues began to slow up, the team began to lose its edge and he seemed somewhat becalmed even going in and out of the Cornwall team.

Things took a big step forward when Cornwall met Surrey (yet again) in a twice replayed semi-final and Stack played three times against England's star prop Tony Horton. Horton apparently sang his praises to the leading rugby writer John Reason who took up the cause of this virtual unknown from the far South West. Nothing happened until 1969 when Cornwall reached the County Final against Lancashire and he got a first England Trial at Hartlepool.

That autumn he was given another trial at Moseley. Stack had a 'blinder' and, having taken the precaution of withdrawing from a Barbarians' invitation to concentrate on the Final Trial, was rewarded with his first 'cap' against South Africa at Twickenham more than a decade after making his bow for the Pirates.

The Springboks were hounded by anti-apartheid demonstrators and the entire tour might well have been cancelled. England won, Stack had a hand in both of the tries and his place seemed secure. Further caps followed against Ireland and Wales but a reverse at

Murrayfield led to him losing his place for the trip to Paris. However he got another call for the Barbarians for their Easter Tour, played against France B at Redruth on same day the full side were in Paris and ended the season with a trip to California with the touring Penguins.

The following year he faced a difficult decision. At twenty-nine he was at his peak and desperately wanted his England place back. He was playing for a club well off the England selectors' radar and even the old route of recognition via county rugby seemed to be tailing off as Cornwall were in decline. He had a family farm to run and couldn't just relocate to Leicester or Coventry like a schoolteacher or a salesman.

He bit the bullet and for a while commuted to London to play for the Harlequins and it seemed to do the trick. He got another game for the Barbarians at Northampton and, following some dismal England defeats, he was recalled to play for England against a World XV brought to Twickenham for the RFU Centenary.

Fortune now smiled upon him. The British Lions were storming through New Zealand like a forest fire and the locals didn't like it one little bit. A vicious match against Canterbury resulted in both McLoughlin and Carmichael being badly hurt and prop reinforcements were called for. Stack found himself on a twenty-six hour flight to the other side of the world and immediately made his debut against Southland at Invercargill.

Although he never quite forced his way into the Test matches he had done extremely well and came back with his reputation sky high. No longer was it necessary to drive hundreds of miles to London and, by keeping himself fit and fresh, he only had to do the necessary when the trials began to be an automatic choice for the next four years. By the time he played his last International in 1975 he had amassed twenty-five caps, had toured South Africa, Fiji and New Zealand again where he scored a vital try in an unexpected England victory. The South Africa trip was also a resounding success as the Springboks were defeated in Johannesburg and Stack had the honour of leading his country in a match against Griqualand West at Kimberley.

His England career coincided with moments of high drama. Following the 'Bloody Sunday' tragedy in Northern Ireland, the Welsh and Scots teams refused to fulfil their fixtures in Dublin. The England players were however made of sterner stuff and the following year, despite veiled threats from the IRA, ran out at Lansdowne Road to a rapturous welcome from thousands of peace-loving Irish rugby fans. Two players had actually withdrawn but Stack was among those who earned the undying respect of all for that display of dignified courage. Nothing terrible happened but nobody was to know that at the time.

Following a drawn game in France in 1974 the England team flew back to London. That very same afternoon a Turkish airliner loaded with rugby supporters and journalists crashed as it left Paris killing all on board. Stack and his colleagues might very easily have been booked onto that flight and rugby's own Munich air disaster was only narrowly avoided. He played in a special England vs France for the victims of this disaster but it did not count as a full international.

That spring he was sounded out about doing a second Lions tour to South Africa but felt that leaving the farm for yet another three month stint was asking too much of those around him.

After his England days ended he continued to play for Cornwall for another couple of years belatedly captaining them for one season and playing against the Wallabies at Exeter.

He remained with the Pirates until he was nearly forty amassing well over 500 matches along the way. The highlight of that latter period was probably his being the lynchpin of the team which won the Cornwall Cup in 1976.

England didn't forget him and he served them again as a selector. He had by then happily played in lower Pirates teams passing on his vast experience to many young lads who were no doubt in awe of him.

In recent years he has sadly suffered from a neurological condition but is naturally very proud of Sam and John his two rugby-playing sons. John of course has been in the back-row with both the Cornish Pirates and Redruth.

# Dave Ward

Position: Hooker/ Flanker
Height/Weight: 5'11", 16st 1lbs
Date of Birth: 1985
Matches: 76 + 34
Tries scored: 24

**Did you know?** Wardy was once selected and had his name appear in the programme for both teams in the same match.

David Patrick Ward was born in Bath where he, his two brothers and sister all grew up in a sporting family. Their father had once been a footballer with Derby County (who continue to be Dave's favourite team) and his mother an excellent tennis player. His father was a pharmaceutical representative in what had by then become a rugby-obsessed city and his sales manager was Malcolm Bell (the father of future Bath and England prop Duncan Bell) and so almost from the cradle it was going to be rugby for young Wardy.

Starting school at St John's Primary, he was going along to Under Six mini rugby and thence progressing up through the age groups. Moving on to The Ridings High School in Bristol his sports horizons widened and he added cricket and 400 metre running to his rugby. Inevitably he was in demand at county level and represented both the Somerset and Bristol teams as a flanker.

He gained a sporting scholarship to Oldfield College which had a rugby academy coached by the ex-Bath and Pirates lock Martin Haag. There was already a Cornish connection in that two fellow students were future Pirates – Simon Whatling and Mike Myerscough. He was soon in the England Schools Under 18 team and gained caps against Wales and Scotland.

By then he had begun switching to hooking and went on to Bath University to study Coach Education and Sports Performance and, while playing there, was recruited by the ex-Bath and England centre John Palmer.

Bath already had two international hookers with both Lee Mears and Jonathan Humphreys in the squad and the ex-Wallaby hooker Michael Foley leading the coaching staff. His opportunities were clearly going to be limited but in 2004 he came on as a replacement against both Treviso and the Saracens.

His first senior start was against mighty Leinster in the Heineken Cup and he found himself directly opposing Shane Byrne who was the current Ireland hooker and possessor of possibly the worst mullet in rugby.

He had two more years at Bath but, however hard he tried, he could not secure a starting place in the team. He got a game against Newcastle in 2006 when he scored a try but was promptly left out again. Indeed it was not until he had been at his present club Harlequins for a few months that he next made a Premiership start thus achieving the unlikely record of a seven-year gap between his first and second Premiership matches.

He was included in the England Under 21 squad to Argentina but, although the squad contained talents of the calibre of Dylan Hartley, James Haskell, Toby Flood and Tom Varndell, the team under-performed and the results were disappointing.

Frustrated at the lack of opportunities, he took the decision to leave his home club Bath and signed for Northampton Saints who had just been relegated to the Championship but were odds-on for an immediate return to the top flight. This seemed a good move but, on reporting for training, he found that the coaching staff who had recruited him had all been sacked. Nevertheless he went into the team for the first five matches and scored four tries including one against the Pirates at Camborne when he faced his future rival Rob Elloway. However after a couple more matches he was then dropped and never regained his place.

The problem was that the new forwards' coach Dorian West and Dave could never see eye-to-eye and consequently his future at Franklins Gardens was effectively doomed.

After a further frustrating spell sat on the side-lines at Sale he contemplated playing part-time with Derby RFC but was then offered full-time opportunities by both Birmingham-Solihull Bees and the Pirates. Fortunately for all concerned he chose the far more ambitious Cornish Pirates.

Suddenly his career seemed to be transformed. Although he found the training surroundings rather basic after having been with three premiership clubs he now experienced what he craved most of all – regular game time.

The new coaching team of Stirling, Biljon and Davies had taken over and he made his debut in the opening friendly against Cardiff and for the next three years rarely missed a match either as the starting hooker, replacement or by occasionally reverting to his old position as a flanker.

It was from the back-row that he set about Munster in the B & I Final when he, Blair Cowan and Chris Morgan made life for the celebrated Irish visitors an absolute nightmare. Ward has no hesitation in rating Morgan as consistently the best forward in the Pirates squad during his time in Cornwall.

Over those three seasons he made some 110 appearances and scored twenty-three tries – a remarkable total for a forward in such a short period. He and Alan Paver formed a spiky duo never happier than when winding up the opposition or causing mayhem at the breakdowns. Indeed his ability to steal the ball either by ripping it away in a maul, tackling the ball as well as an opponent or turning it over on the ground at a breakdown was something he developed into some sort of mystical art form. Inevitably this led to quite a few penalties and yellow cards against him from incredulous referees who could never quite fathom out what he had actually done.

The team under Stirling was probably the strongest ever assembled by the Pirates and they reached the Championship playoffs for two years running. Soon there was interest from Premiership clubs and he initially agreed on a move to London Irish but this was never completed. Just before the second Playoff Final an offer from Harlequins came in at the very same moment as the imminent hopes for the Stadium for Cornwall were being dashed yet again. This time he moved on.

Success did not come overnight as he found himself third choice behind Gray and Buchanan but the Quins coaching staff were both encouraging and optimistic. He worked away at his one relative Achilles heel – his throwing in to the line-out – and in season 2013/14 everything came right all of a sudden. His two rivals were both injured and he grabbed the opportunity with both hands. His ball-stealing exploits left TV commentators purring in appreciation and he picked up no less than five Man of the Match awards in a matter of a few weeks.

It was not long before he was chosen for the England Saxons and, with a close season England tour to New Zealand coming up, many pundits saw him as a dark horse for the England team itself. Dave made the party but, with Webber recovering from injury, he only made one replacement appearance against the Crusaders but still loved the experience.

He continues as an integral part of Conor O'Shea's exciting team working with their front row guru John Kingston. Despite a period of injury, he was the Quins' main hooker last season and finished it by becoming a Barbarian and hooking against the ex-Pirate Junior Luke Cowan-Dickie who was in an England XV. He has also taken on being the Head Coach of the Guildford club having started his coaching journey back in Cornwall at St Just.

He has very fond memories of Cornwall and the people at the Pirates and returns frequently. He recalls being housed in the smallest room he had ever seen in a tiny flat across the road from the Mennaye which he shared with three other young Pirate players.

Another abiding memory of Pirate fans was of minding his own business shopping in Tesco when a loud voice boomed out across the aisles, 'Oi Wardy when are you going to sort out your bleddy throwing boy?', as he tried desperately to hide behind the rows of tinned soup.

# John White

Position: Flanker
Height/Weight: 5' 10", 13st 0lbs
Date of Birth: 1944
Matches: 320
Tries: 27

**Did you know?** John was called back from his honeymoon in Scotland to play a match for Cornwall.

Nicholas John White was born in Pendeen during the war. His father Nicky had a large dairy farm out by the coast and that is where John and his two sisters grew up. His father had played on the wing for Newlyn before the war but there was more family interest in horses than there was in rugby.

He started school at St Erbyn's and at the age of nine began to play the game for the first time alongside future Pirates such as John Skewes, Mike Bolitho, John Tellam and Geoffrey Lawry. There was no mini rugby or equivalent at the time and the boys were introduced by headmaster Rex Carr and a schoolmaster and part-time local cricket journalist named Michael Williams directly into the full game in which John invariably turned out at fly-half.

At thirteen he went to Kelly College at Tavistock which was a well-known rugby school although John concentrated more upon swimming and boxing. In fact although he played the game he never even got into his school team. He had planned to join the Navy but, having been away at Kelly for four years, a serious accident to his father required him to come home and look after the farm.

The Pirates had a prop forward at the time called Bill Butters who was a baker at Pendeen and it was he who used to drive John into training with the Mounts Bay Colts. It was there under the guidance of Ken Thomas that John finally caught the rugby 'bug' for the first time. He was already seventeen but had two seasons with the Colts alongside regular future Pirate colleagues Roger Pascoe, Mike Thomas and Keith Stirling. He was bitterly disappointed not to be selected for Cornwall Colts having felt he had outplayed the selected flanker during the trial match.

In season 1962–63 he moved up to senior rugby and, after a few matches for the Reserves, made his debut against Truro in late October. He was by now settled as an open-side flanker and the opposing fly-half was the future Cornwall and Gloucester stalwart Tommy Palmer but John did well enough to put himself into contention for a place in Gerald Luke's powerful team. The competition was fierce with Brian Monckton, Fudge Trudgeon and Bez Berryman comprising the regular back-row trio but John nevertheless managed five matches that season.

Life for amateur players like John and Stack Stevens who earn their livings as cattle farmers could sometimes be difficult. On several occasions he had to dash off from a match before he could even take a shower in order to get back to Pendeen in time to milk his cows. Indeed his life was a decidedly hectic one. His other sport was point-to-point racing and on one crazy occasion he won the infamous Ding Dong race in the morning, played for the Pirates against St Ives in the afternoon, did the milking and then had to rush off having learned that his son had just fallen off a wall playing at teammate Tony Stevenson's house and fractured his skull. Fortunately the lad made a complete recovery.

He began the next season back in the Reserves but his breakthrough came in the November when he was brought in for a match with St Ives and scored the winning try. That match was probably the making of John and he was henceforward a regular in the side and this was further cemented when Trudgeon decided to emigrate to Canada early in the New Year.

For the next few years he was an automatic selection for the team and stood out in a side which candidly was no longer of the quality it had been a few seasons earlier. It is always difficult to shine in these circumstances but, although the Pirates suffered some heavy defeats, he was invariably tearing about the field tackling his heart out.

Even at the time he was considered to be on the small side but he had raw pace, was naturally fit, had good handling skills and above all an unbreakable spirit. Had he been in a stronger team he would undoubtedly have received far more honours than he actually did.

Cornwall was blessed with several outstanding flankers at the time in Ray George (whom John reckoned to be his hardest opponent), Gerry McKeown and later Peter Hendy. As a result John probably received more Travelling Reserve cards for Cornwall than anyone could ever remember. In the modern days of multiple replacements he would undoubtedly have appeared in dozens of matches for the county team.

When he did make his debut in September 1967 at Camborne it was against a powerful Crawshay's team containing six Welsh internationals in the pack and he found himself facing the British Lions fly-half Dai Watkins. John was suffering from flu and probably should not have played but was naturally desperate to do so. Against all the odds, Cornwall forced a highly creditable draw and Watkins did very little. It was all so tense that by half-time John's flu had miraculously disappeared.

He was brought back in for the game with Devon at Devonport when both McKeown and George withdrew and Cornwall won their only game of the year. The next match with Gloucestershire was postponed due to a foot-and-mouth epidemic and by the time it was finally played McKeown was back and available.

The following September he faced Sussex in Penzance and promptly smashed his jaw. In fact he suffered badly from injuries throughout his career including at least four broken noses, a knee operation and being nearly killed by blood poisoning after sustaining a cut chin on a pitch at St Austell which had been sprayed with some form of toxic fertiliser.

In 1970 he took over the captaincy from Alf Fowler late in the season and was to lead the club in his own right twice more. The first time was in 1972 when he only lasted three matches before the dreaded injury curse struck yet again and he was ruled out for the rest of the season. The next year went very much better and he led the team without interruption.

The highlight of the latter part of his Pirate career was undoubtedly the Cornwall Cup win over Redruth in 1976. By this time his back-row colleagues were Dumbo Dymond and Phil Westren and John once again defended valiantly as the Pirates were determined there should be no repeat of the disappointing final of the previous year – a game in which John had also featured.

Soon afterwards he had two years playing for St Just but was called back for a cup tie against Redruth in early 1978 but that was to be the end. St Just had actually played their very first match against a Pirates invitation team on a pitch marked out on John's own farm at Trewellard near Pendeen.

He did a short stint helping with the coaching at the Pirates but by then he and his wife Sue had taken a farmhouse at St Hilary and had begun what soon became a flourishing high quality guest house. He spent many years driving lorries between Penzance and the West Midlands and then coming back to work all hours supporting his wife in the bed and breakfast business.

His son Ben played schoolboy rugby at a high level also as a flanker and had several games for the Pirates.

He actually played in one more special game arranged to celebrate Roger Pascoe's thousand matches for the Pirates but found himself crashing into a rock hard young Adrian Bick and sensibly concluded that playing rugby was probably no longer such a good idea.

# Alvin Williams

Position: Lock
Height/Weight: 6'2", 16st 5lbs
Date of Birth: 1933
Matches: 817 (751 first team)
Tries: 27

**Did you know?** Alvin achieved all his ball-handling skills and sporting success despite being blinded in one eye due to a childhood accident.

Alvin Williams was born in Penzance as the son of a merchant seaman. He went to St Paul's Junior School and then to the Penzance Grammar but actually played no rugby until he was fifteen years old. He was good at sport in general with athletics, cross country and swimming all competing with football where he played in goal and supported the Magpies.

When Cardiff came to town in 1948 he sneaked over the fence and what he saw fascinated him. The Grammar School did not yet play rugby but, with Pirate stalwarts Ben Batten and Fred Jarvis on the staff, he followed many of his classmates to play for the burgeoning Under 16 Colts team and then progressed to the Under 18 Mounts Bay side. He was already a big strapping lad and showed such an aptitude for the game that he, together with fellow colts Jim Matthews and Gerald Luke, gained a place in the England Air Training Corps international match against Scotland at Edinburgh. He also went to Hanover in Germany with the Cornwall Schools team.

Alvin was already showing great promise as a powerful swimmer and indeed throughout his rugby career he was a major force in his summer sport of water polo at which he captained Penzance, St Lukes College and Cornwall for many years. He was also a very useful basketball player and represented the South West in that as well.

Cornish rugby forwards always had a reputation for being tough, fit and physically hard but they were seldom very big. Indeed, when compared with the towering line-out kings of modern rugby, Alvin at only a couple of inches over 6 feet would have been considered a midget and would probably have had to have made his career as a prop. In his own era he was actually considered to be a big hefty item. Even so he often gave away several inches to the international second-row forwards of the time which perhaps prevented him getting even higher recognition. However his athleticism, aggression, water polo handling skills and fitness allowed him to be a highly competitive front jumper despite this obvious handicap.

In Feb 1951 he made his senior debut for the club as a rangy seventeen-year-old lock against the R. N. E. College from Manadon on a day when two Pirates were away playing for England in Dublin. Young Alvin did well and got further opportunities by the end of the season against Exeter, Gloucester and Pontypridd which must have been a steep learning experience.

His appearances for the Pirates First XV were spasmodic for the next couple of years although he did have two outstanding games against Redruth and the Wasps and broke into Harvey Richards's long-unbeaten team as the 1953 season drew to a close.

This absence was due to the fact that he was now studying to qualify as a teacher at St Luke's College in Exeter. That team in 1953/54 was packed with a galaxy of young Welsh Internationals including Bryn Meredith, Glyn John, Gareth Griffiths, Don Devereux and Brian Sparks as well as his fellow Pirates Derek Small and Johnny Thomas. They carried all before them, were unbeaten throughout the entire season and scored over 1,000 points which was an incredible feat given that a try was then only worth three points and there were no goal-kicking tees.

Alvin played a major role in this all-conquering team and during his Easter holidays he played at Number 8 for the Pirates against a star-studded Cardiff team lined up in opposition to a current darling of Welsh rugby called Sid Judd.

The following year Cornwall reached the semi-finals for the first time since the war and, although not part of that team, he had made his Cornwall debut against the British Police at Camborne earlier in the season. Soon he became an automatic selection for Cornwall over the next decade amassing fifty county caps in the process. Initially he packed down alongside Camborne's renowned tough nut Gary Harris and latterly with the Pirates' own David Mann.

His time with Cornwall coincided with an era when they reached the Final against a brilliant Warwickshire team at Coventry in 1958 having first overcome a powerful Lancashire team in front of 20,000 ecstatic supporters at Redruth. Having gone into a lead, Cornwall battled through falling snow but despite the valiant efforts of Alvin, Vic Roberts, Bonzo Johns and the other Cornish heroes, the Midlanders packed with England players finally won the day.

That season he was also selected alongside Harris to play for a combined Devon and Cornwall team at Plymouth Argyle's Home Park in a drawn match against the touring Wallabies.

Two years later he was running out at Twickenham for a close semi-final against Surrey and in 1962 went back to Coventry for his third and last semi-final. Cornwall again fought hard but, up against two giant England locks in Tom Pargetter and Colin Payne, Alvin and the aforesaid David Mann had a tough afternoon of it and again Warwickshire went on to take the title.

The previous year Alvin had played one of the games of his life against the Springboks at Camborne. The Boks had a couple of huge 'meanies' in their second-row called Piet Van Zyl and Stompie Van der Merwe but time and again he cleaned them out. The tourists finally won a thrilling match but Alvin had battled for every ball as if his life depended upon it and if ever he was going to catch the eyes of England selectors this was surely the moment. Sadly it was not to be.

Since leaving St Luke's he had begun teaching at Pool Secondary School where he continued for some forty years and introduced rugby. In the amateur days sports teaching was a favourite job for Pirates players and he had an astonishing run in the team over the next seventeen years captaining the club in 1960–61, 1964–65 and 1967–68 (he only missed a match with Redruth due to getting married) while amassing an incredible 817 matches in a Pirate shirt – a figure unimaginable in today's environment. Even when not captain, he was very much an on-field leader and many young forwards learned a great deal from playing alongside him.

It was not uncommon in those days for lock-forwards to be entrusted with goal-kicking and Alvin was always happy to step up and oblige. Perhaps he was no Jonny Wilkinson but he nevertheless landed a huge number of vital penalties and conversions whenever called upon.

After playing his last match against Tredegar in 1973, some twenty-two years after his debut, he continued to serve the game he loved. He became a popular referee on the Cornwall and Devon circuit, and as the ultimate poacher-turned-gamekeeper, he was due no little respect. That cannot always have been the case as on one occasion in 1975 he reached the national newspapers for having sent off seven players in a single match between Falmouth and Bideford. He refereed for ten years during which he took the whistle for numerous first-class club and county matches.

He later became President of the Pirates from 1987–90 as well as fixture secretary and did much to hold things together when the club went through some of its worst ever times on the pitch.

In 1967 he had married Jackie and they had three sons of whom two, Nick and Ross, represented the Pirates. Nick was a big strong prop who played for several seasons with the Pirates and for Cornwall. He also featured in at least a couple of matches where Alvin was the referee. Their on field conversations regarding scrummaging offences must have been fascinating.

He now devotes his time more to property development, travelling and a bit of golf at Cape Cornwall.

# John 'Ginger' Williams

Position: Centre
Height/Weight: 5' 11" 13st 0lbs
Date of Birth: 1927
Died: 2000
Matches: 125
Tries: 36

**Did you know?** Ginger Williams once invited a team under his own name to take on the Pirates and then played against his own team.

John Michael Williams was the younger and smaller of two brothers who played a huge part in the early post-war history of Penzance & Newlyn RFC. He was a well-built young man with a thatch of reddish hair which led to his inevitable nickname of 'Ginger'. This proved useful to differentiate him from another J. Williams (known as 'Jack') who sometimes appeared in a similar position for the Pirates at the time and their playing records are consequently often difficult to untangle.

He was born in Penzance and, as with his brother Nicky and so many of his time, was introduced to rugby by headmaster Rex Carr while at St Erbyns School. Their uncle was the celebrated Lieutenant-Colonel J. H. Williams (known as 'Elephant Bill') who found fame writing of his wartime exploits fighting the Japanese with the creative use of elephants in the jungles of Burma. Early in that war John followed his brother to Rugby School and it was there that he blossomed as a thrusting centre albeit with a slightly ungainly running style.

On leaving school he was drafted into the Army and was in due course commissioned as a Second-Lieutenant in the Guards. He made his debut for the Pirates in November 1945 at Falmouth and thereafter played intermittently for the rest of the season. He did however make the side for the big match of the year against Cardiff and scored a try to cap it off.

Earlier in the winter he was perhaps surprisingly selected for the combined Cornwall and Devon team to face the New Zealand Army side which was touring the country under the name of the Kiwis. This was made up of serving New Zealanders still over in Europe and, although not an official All Blacks team, was almost of Test Match strength. The game took place at Torquay in February and although he had yet to be selected for Cornwall Ginger had an outstanding match.

This was put right in April when he took part in a 'friendly' against Devon at bomb-scarred Plymouth. Some of his early matches for the club were in his favoured position of centre but he frequently was selected at fly-half to partner Trevor Nicholls as the new club struggled to establish itself.

In 1947 his elder brother was elected club captain, the Wallabies arrived in Penzance and Ginger began a famous centre three-quarter partnership with the spectacular Mike Terry. For the next five years they were a pairing to be admired and feared and crowds flocked to the Mennaye just to see them. Selectors did strange things in those days and, although both turned out for Cornwall on numerous occasions, it was not until the early mid-1950s that they actually picked them to play together. To be fair they had the England centre Keith Scott and the brilliant British Lion Malcolm Thomas available but it was still curious.

He then went to Clare College in Cambridge and won his 'Blue' in 1949 when he lined up directly opposite Oxford's England star centre Lewis Cannell. Ginger's team lost narrowly by a single and rather lucky try to nil.

In December 1950 both he and Terry were selected for the opening England trial at Otley. Ginger was in his accustomed position in the centre but Terry was perversely banished to the wing. Ginger retained his place for all three trials and, although not being selected for the disastrous opening match at Swansea, was brought into the side for the game against Ireland in Dublin alongside Coventry's Ivor Preece. Again England lost and he was omitted when France came to Twickenham.

With a French victory and England facing an embarrassing whitewash he was recalled for the match with Scotland in a team led by Kendall-Carpenter and which also included Penryn's Vic Roberts for what is still the only occasion since before the First World War for three Cornishmen to be in an England team together. England squeaked a win and honour was saved – but Ginger's career as an International was already over. He nevertheless returned to Twickenham a month later to play for the Pirates in the Middlesex Sevens.

The next season he was available back in Cornwall and was elected captain of the club. In early October he was in the South West Counties team against the Springboks at Home Park, Plymouth. The locals matched the Boks at a single try apiece but lost the match to the boot of their goal-kicking prop 'Okey' Geffin. He also played in every Cornwall match scoring a fine try against Devon at Exeter. In that year when he was captain he managed to play thirty-five games and completed the season playing as an emergency flanker against Gloucester.

By the next season his work as a solicitor had taken him to London where he was to play for Richmond for the rest of his career. Before he did so he initiated something which became a tradition which was to bring a powerful team of International and other leading players to take on the Pirates in one of the opening matches of the season.

In April he pulled on a Pirate shirt for the very last time when he came back to face Cardiff and the might of Dr Jack Matthews, Gareth Griffiths and Cliff Morgan so he certainly went out at the top. At the end of that season he returned to Twickenham for the Middlesex Sevens and this time was part of a team which won the trophy. He had also been made a Barbarian by playing on their Easter tour against both Cardiff and Newport.

He had continued to play regularly for Cornwall and in December 1953 he was at last paired with his old comrade-in-arms Mike Terry in the centre for the South West against the All Blacks at Camborne. They did well enough but the tourists claimed their usual win.

The highlight of his career in the Cornwall team came a year later when the South West group was won and Berkshire defeated to set up a semi-final with Middlesex at Redruth. Terry had gone abroad with the army but he now had the young Penryn and Northampton man Roger Hosen alongside him.

Hosen was then a raw talent with a kick like a howitzer and it was Ginger's job to try to coax both him and the new Pirate star Gerald Luke through the big match. Behind the scrum Middlesex had the two current England halves plus the experienced Nim Hall and the explosive Ted Woodward and it was they who finally turned the tide in favour of the Londoners.

By this time he had been made captain of Richmond who were then one of the leading clubs in the country and he was generally acknowledged to have been one of the best they had ever appointed and so was immediately re-elected for a second season.

He played his twenty-fifth and last match for Cornwall against Gloucestershire at Redruth on the same afternoon that his friend Kendall-Carpenter also decided to call a halt to his county rugby. In April 1957 he finally hung up his boots to concentrate upon his business career.

He had married into the Holman family who were then the major employer in Camborne with their compressor and rock drill businesses. Ginger worked his passage up through the firm becoming a director in due course. He kept in close touch with rugby and continued to bring his 'J. M. Williams International XV' each September to play not only the Pirates but also Redruth when he invariably acted not only as host but as touch judge as well.

His teams always contained exciting players – none more so than the magnificent Tony O'Reilly and Lions' captain Arthur Smith who once scored five tries in a rather one-sided encounter on the Mennaye.

He continued to enjoy golf and his other great love of sailing and died aged seventy-three at Budock on the Helford River in September 2000. His elder brother rose to become Chairman and Managing Director of Burmah Castrol.

# Steve Winn

Position: Centre
Height/Weight: 6' 0", 14st 0lbs
Date of Birth: 1978
Matches: 88 + 45
Tries: 15

**Did you know?** Steve has recently become a keen competitor in 'Tough Mudder' challenge events.

Although Steve Winn was born in Bridgend he is very much a man of Maesteg – a true Welsh rugby town with traditions not unlike those at Redruth. His father once played as a flanker for a local club called Maesteg Celtic where he is still an active member.

As a result Steve was steeped in rugby from an early age playing mini and junior rugby for another local club called Maesteg Welsh for whom he made his senior debut at the tender age of sixteen. At school he was an outstanding centre gaining caps for Wales at Under 16, Under 18 and Under 19 levels in several cases a year early. He also did well at athletics achieving county honours both in sprint events and throwing the javelin.

It was soon evident that he should be playing at a higher level and at seventeen he joined Bridgend who had a good set of backs and, even more importantly for Steve, some highly competent coaches. Before long he was gaining further honours for Wales in Under 21 and Wales A matches and also representing them in Sevens. In the Under 21 side he played outside the future Pirate fly-half Lee Jarvis whose opposite number when they played against England was a young Jonny Wilkinson.

He had about sixty-five matches for Bridgend spread over three seasons and then got a better offer to play for Swansea where he continued for a further three years. It seemed only a matter of time before he would be called upon for Wales itself but he was dogged by bad luck. Having been selected, a shoulder injury required an operation which ruled him out of a trip to play in South Africa. Lightning seemed to strike twice when he again withdrew through injury having been asked to accompany Wales to Argentina. He finally did get to go with the Development team to Canada but once again managed only forty minutes of actual rugby. Sadly that coveted 'cap' always seemed to elude him.

When Swansea linked up with Neath to form the Ospreys, Steve found himself looking for another club. He was not short of offers and immediately joined the Gwent Dragons. By coincidence he made his debut for them in a pre-season friendly against the Pirates in August 2003 just after their promotion to National One. The Dragons ran riot and won by 53-8 and Steve notched a hat-trick of tries. Their back line that afternoon included no less than five men who would all find their way to the Pirates in due course.

After a couple of years he found that his face did not seem to fit with the Dragons' coach and he started to look for another club. The link to the Pirates was made by their CEO David Jenkins and after a call from Dicky Evans he decided to leave Wales and come down to Cornwall.

After his debut against Ebbw Vale he opposed his former teammates in another pre-season friendly and soon established himself in the side working alongside either of the two Duncans – Roke or Bell. He found himself coming off the bench during the EDF Trophy winning run and his appearance at Twickenham was again as a replacement although he was able to share in the burst of joy at the final whistle. In all he made nineteen starts in that first season with another seven as a replacement.

The following season he only managed to really establish himself as a first choice by the late autumn but then struck up a close working relationship with ex-Rugby League man Paul Devlin. Both had accumulated a wealth of experience and brought a considerable degree of thought into their rugby as opposed to the mere 'crash bang' approach which characterised so many back lines in the Championship at the time and indeed does to this day.

One of their best days together was in November 2008 at Bedford when, after a rather indifferent run of games, the Pirates clicked suddenly into gear and Steve capped a fine personal display by running away to score the decisive try deep into the second half.

If he had been disappointed not to have made the starting selection at Twickenham, things were very much rosier when Munster came to Camborne for the B & I Final. Playing outside the brilliant Jonny Bentley, Steve showed all his old guile in claiming a superb try under the posts and then leading a defensive assault on the young Irishmen whenever they threatened to force their way back into the match.

It is probably for his tireless and clinical defensive work that Steve will be best remembered by Pirate devotees. Although clearly not quite as quick as he had been as a youngster, his organisation and timing of the defensive line was an example to all aspiring midfielders at the club. The following season, which in fact turned out to be Steve's last, he was instrumental in getting the best out of the more flamboyant skills of Matt Hopper.

Whereas Matt was all bursts, sidesteps and rushing up to pressurise the opposition, Steve would repeatedly be found just behind him tidying up and cutting down opponents who had somehow survived the younger man's headlong crash tackles. It was something which played a big part in the Pirates having their best overall season and going all the way to the Championship Finals.

This was perhaps best illustrated in late October when the Pirates surprised and delighted their supporters by shading Worcester Warriors at Sixways. Working alongside Hopper, the two Pirate centres shut down their opposite numbers Rasmussen and Short so effectively that a furious Andy Goode got himself yellow carded through sheer frustration. It was a moment and a match that Winny would have savoured.

Ironically he had very nearly left the club at the end of the previous season after the Munster game. The Pirates were seeking to maximise their playing budget by having as many members as possible able to cover several positions. Steve was a specialist centre (who had occasionally been pressed into service as a replacement flanker in an emergency) and, nearing thirty-three, might have been let go. He considered offers from Brett Davey at Doncaster and Graham Dawe at Plymouth but happily the Pirates stepped back in and the Winn and Hopper relationship was thus born.

By the end of his final year Drew Locke had forced his way into the side and as a result Steve missed out on the Playoff Finals. He had a house and a young family in Hayle but the call of a return to his homeland of South Wales was a strong one. He had a season as a professional with a club called Tonmawr who are situated in the Neath valley as a feeder club for the Ospreys. He then moved back to Bridgend, where his senior career had once begun, acting very much as the senior professional and a mentor to younger players.

Today he has trained to work in a home for children who have been taken into care often after having suffered from severe ill treatment. This is clearly very valuable work and he derives a lot of satisfaction from it although it is a round-the-clock job which is often both physically and emotionally demanding.

His son Harry is a promising young footballer and has already been spotted by Cardiff City and Swansea while Steve himself keeps in trim with weight training and a bit of boxing.

Twickenham EDF Winners